INTERNATIONAL DEBT AND THE STABILITY OF THE WORLD ECONOMY

William R. Cline

POLICY ANALYSES IN INTERNATIONAL ECONOMICS 4

INSTITUTE FOR INTERNATIONAL ECONOMICS

WASHINGTON, DC

SEPTEMBER 1983

William R. Cline is a Senior Fellow at the Institute for International Economics. He was formerly a Senior Fellow at the Brookings Institution; Deputy Director for Development and Trade Research at the US Treasury Department; Ford Foundation Visiting Professor at the Instituto de Planejamento Econômico e Social Aplicado (IPEA) in Brazil; Assistant Professor at Princeton University; and is currently Professorial Lecturer at Johns Hopkins University School for Advanced International Studies. Dr. Cline has published many books and articles on international trade, finance, and development, including two earlier POLICY ANALYSES *released by the Institute:* "Reciprocity": A New Approach to World Trade Policy? *and (with C. Fred Bergsten)* Trade Policy in the 1980s.

David Johnson provided invaluable research assistance for this study. For helpful comments, I am grateful to C. Fred Bergsten, Richard N. Cooper, Carlos Diaz-Alejandro, Chandra Hardy, John R. Petty, Nicholas Sargen, Mario Henrique Simonsen, Ernest Stern, Ralph Tryon, and participants in seminars presented at Chase Manhattan Bank, the Federal Reserve Bank of New York, and the World Bank.

INSTITUTE FOR INTERNATIONAL ECONOMICS
C. Fred Bergsten, *Director*
Kathleen A. Lynch, *Director of Publications*
Rosanne Gleason, *Publications Assistant*

The Institute for International Economics was created, and is principally funded, by the German Marshall Fund of the United States.

The views expressed in this publication are those of the author. The publication is part of the research program of the Institute, as endorsed by its Board of Directors, but does not necessarily reflect the views of individual members of the Board or the Advisory Committee.

Printed in the United States of America
89 88 87   6 5 4

Library of Congress Cataloging in Publications Data
Cline, William R.
  International debt and the stability of the world
economy.
  (Policy analyses in international economics; 4)

  1. Loans, Foreign—Developing countries, 2. Debts,
External—Developing countries. I. Title. II. Series.
HJ8899.C54 1983   336.3'435'091724   83-12888
ISBN 0-88132-010-2
ISBN 0-262-53048-1 (MIT Press)

Contents

Preface

This publication attempts to present a comprehensive analysis of one of the most important and complex problems facing the world economy: the debt crisis. In an effort to achieve the Institute's objective of making its work available to a wide audience, the study summarizes quite briefly, in footnotes and annexes, much of the technical analysis underlying its findings and conclusions. For economists and others interested in the complete methodology used, and more elaborate presentation of the underlying data and country cases, the Institute will shortly publish a more detailed volume entitled *International Debt: Systemic Risk and Policy Response*, also by William R. Cline. This technique of publishing a shorter policy-oriented version and a longer, more detailed version of the same study follows the approach previously developed in our work on *IMF Conditionality* and *Trade Policy in the 1980s*.

The Institute for International Economics is a private nonprofit research institution for the study and discussion of international economic policy. Its purpose is to analyze important issues in that area, and to develop and communicate practical new approaches for dealing with them.

The Institute was created in November 1981 through a generous commitment of funds from the German Marshall Fund of the United States. Financial support has been received from other private foundations and corporations. The Institute is completely nonpartisan.

The Board of Directors bears overall responsibility for the Institute and gives general guidance and approval to its research program—including identification of topics that are likely to become important to international economic policymakers over the medium run (generally, one to three years) and which thus should be addressed by the Institute. The Director of the Institute, working closely with the staff and outside Advisory Committee, is responsible for the development of particular projects and makes the final decision to publish an individual study.

The Institute hopes that its studies and other activities will contribute to building a stronger foundation for international economic policy around the world. Comments as to how it can best do so are invited from readers of these publications.

C. FRED BERGSTEN
Director

Introduction

Analysts have kept a wary eye on the growing external debt of developing countries since at least the early 1970s. External debt has always been an instrument with both positive potential for economic development and associated risk of financial strain. In the normal course of world development, capital should flow from advanced countries, where it is abundant and its return is relatively low, to developing countries, where capital is scarce and its return high. Direct investment is one form of this capital flow, but since the 1970s it has been far overshadowed by financial capital, especially in the form of bank loans to middle-income countries.

While these flows have contributed to development, they have also meant increasing financial dependence of borrowing countries and rising relative debt-servicing obligations. They therefore set the stage for financial strains if, because of international recession, commodity price collapse, or domestic mismanagement, a country cannot meet the original terms of its debt servicing. In the 1960s and early 1970s, episodes of debt-servicing difficulty often were viewed as another variant on the need for development assistance (and in some cases, such as India and Pakistan, intentional debt restructuring was even used as an aid vehicle). Beginning in the mid-1970s, however, the sheer volume of external debt began to reach such magnitudes that potential disruptions in debt servicing posed a threat not only for a country's development but also for the international financial system, and the banks in particular. Yet international lending in the 1970s continued to confound the pessimists, as relatively smooth expansion of lending achieved financial ''recycling,'' the channeling of surpluses from oil-exporting countries to oil-importing countries in deficit, after the oil shock of 1974.

By 1980–81, evidence of strain on the system was increasing, however. World recession, high interest rates, and a second oil shock took their toll. Near default in Poland shook the credit markets. Then, in 1982–83 the debt problem became manifest and widespread. All three of the largest developing-country debtors—Brazil, Mexico, and Argentina—were forced to disrupt normal debt servicing. Debt-servicing disruption or formal reschedulings of debt reached approximately two-thirds of bank debt owed by the developing and East European countries (section 2). By the end of 1982, 34 countries were in arrears on their debt.[1] The amounts of debt formally rescheduled rose from $2.6 billion in 1981 to $5.5 billion in 1982[2] to approximately $90 billion (including amounts being renegotiated) in 1983.[3]

Public policy on international debt now stands at a turning point. The debt issue has played an increasing role in economic policy formation, apparently affecting decisions such as the major shift by the US Federal Reserve toward faster monetary growth and lower nominal interest rates in the summer of 1982, as well as the change in the US administration's position on raising resources available to the International Monetary Fund.[4] Exposure of industrial economies to risk from the debt of developing countries has added a wholly new dimension to the effects of international economic interdependence, a phenomenon already of growing importance in recent decades through the more familiar channels of trade and monetary relationships.

Yet despite the clear attention the debt problem is now receiving from policymakers internationally, it remains unclear whether the financial emergencies that surfaced in 1982–83 will be resolved by the various rescue packages already in place. Some analysts and statesmen argue that the debt problem has become so severe that it cannot be managed using past approaches, and that broad new schemes of debt relief are required. In contrast, official statements of international organizations tend to downplay the risk of debt to the international financial system.[5] Despite such assurances, doubt remains about the extent of this risk. Even the most straightforward policy remedies stir heated controversy that the public is bailing out the banks. And, while

---

1. According to a 15 February 1983 communication with the International Monetary Fund.

2. World Bank, *World Debt Tables,* 1982–83 ed., p. 2.

3. M.S. Mendelsohn, *Commercial Banks and the Restructuring of Cross-Border Debt* (New York: Group of Thirty, 1983), p. 4.

4. As recommended in John Williamson, *The Lending Policies of the International Monetary Fund,* POLICY ANALYSES IN INTERNATIONAL ECONOMICS 1 (Washington: Institute for International Economics, August 1982).

5. Thus, the World Bank takes "an unfashionably positive view of the external indebtedness of developing countries" and maintains that "There is no generalized debt crisis...," World Bank, *World Debt Tables,* 1982–83 ed., pp. vii, xvi.

much of public attention is focused on the risks of a debt crisis for the banking system, a quiet crisis already exists in the severe economic recession being confronted by many developing countries, in large part because of their adverse balance of payments positions and debt burden.

The debt problem not only poses potential risk for the international financial system; in addition, it has already contributed to reduced exports and jobs in industrial countries as developing countries have retrenched on their imports. Including members of the Organization of Petroleum Exporting Countries (OPEC), developing countries account for 40 percent of US exports and 42 percent of European Community (EC) exports to non-EC markets. From 1981 to 1982 exports of OECD countries to non-OPEC developing-country nonmembers declined by $14 billion in real terms, an amount corresponding to approximately 350,000 jobs.[6] Resolution of the debt problem can contribute directly to recovery in industrial countries in addition to reducing the risk of a much larger economic dislocation from international financial collapse.

This study examines the major areas of public policy on external debt. Section 1 analyzes the origins of the debt problem. Section 2 examines the potential risk to industrial-country economies and financial systems (primarily through their banks) posed by the debt of developing and East European countries, and reviews the important series of debt packages orchestrated by the International Monetary Fund, the US government, and other official actors in 1982 responding to financial crisis in Mexico, Brazil, Argentina, and certain other countries.

Section 3 presents a model for projecting the debt and balance of payments of the large debtor countries. This analysis focuses on the fundamental question: is the debt problem a manageable one of short-term illiquidity, or is it so entrenched that it represents country insolvency that must be dealt with by radical measures? In answering this question the level of world economic growth plays the largest role. Section 4 analyzes the dynamics of "involuntary lending" under current circumstances, the technical aspects of debt rescheduling, and the calculus of default decisions.

Today's debt problem is intimately linked to banking institutions, and section 5 examines the adequacy of these institutions (including bank

---

6. The decline was from $220 billion to $196 billion, of which a part was attributable to a 4 percent reduction in dollar prices of exports. OECD *Monthly Statistics of Foreign Trade,* June 1983, pp. 37, 42, 49; and International Monetary Fund, *International Financial Statistics,* June 1983, p. 56.

regulation). In section 6 the projections of this study are matched against prospective levels of international financing to examine the feasibility of global debt management over the medium term. Section 7 examines some of the plans that have been proposed for more radical debt relief as a solution to the debt problem, as well as a general contingency strategy. The policy conclusions of this study are summarized, and concrete recommendations in several areas set forth, in section 8.

1   Origins of the Problem

The global debt problem stems from forces dating to the mid-1970s, and the first oil price shock (1973–74) in particular. The intensification of the problem in 1982 derived primarily from the effects of global recession from 1980 to 1982, combined with adverse psychological shocks to credit markets caused by events in individual major countries. In a broad sense the problem is a consequence of the transition from inflation to disinflation in the world economy. Funds that were borrowed when inflation was high and real interest rates were low or negative are no longer cheap in an environment of lower inflation and high real interest rates.

Debt Trends

The large magnitude and rapid growth of international debt is shown in table 1. For the "nonoil" developing countries (including such new oil exporters as Mexico and Egypt) total debt (including short-term) multiplied nearly fivefold from 1973 to 1982, reaching approximately $612 billion. The estimated debt of five OPEC countries that are not in capital surplus—Algeria, Ecuador, Indonesia, Nigeria, and Venezuela—adds another $80 billion, and net East European debt (in hard currency) accounts for another $53 billion (excluding the Soviet Union).[7] The total debt of these three groups of countries thus stood at approximately $745 billion at the end of 1982.

The bulk of this external debt is sovereign debt: amounts owed abroad by national governments, by their decentralized agencies, or by private firms but with public guarantees. However, a considerable portion of the debt is owed by the private sector without public guarantee. The World Bank estimates that 80 percent of long-term developing-country debt was public

---

7. The estimates of debt used in this study are described in Appendix A. East European debt: *Wall Street Journal*, 4 April 1983 and Wharton Econometric Forecasting Associates.

TABLE 1   **Indicators of external debt, nonoil developing countries, 1973–82**
(billion dollars and percentages)

	1973	1974	1975	1976	1977
External debt					
Total	130.1	160.8	190.8	228.0	278.5
Long-term	118.8	138.1	163.5	194.9	235.9
Total, 1975 prices[a]	169.0	175.7	190.8	218.0	250.9
Exports[b]	112.7	153.7	155.9	181.7	220.3
Debt/exports (percentage)	115.4	104.6	122.4	125.5	126.4
Debt service[c]/exports (percentage)					
Reported	15.9	14.4	16.1	15.3	15.4
Adjusted[d]	n.a.	− 1.6	6.5	10.5	9.4
Debt/GDP (percentage)	22.4	21.8	23.8	25.7	27.4
Oil as percentage of					
Imports[e]	5.9	12.6	13.3	15.6	15.1

n.a. Not available.
Source: IMF, *World Economic Outlook,* 1982 and 1983.
a. Deflating by US wholesale prices.
b. Goods and services.
c. Includes interest (but not amortization) on short-term debt.
d. Deducting inflationary erosion of debt.
e. Net oil importers only.

or publicly guaranteed in 1981, and 20 percent was private.[8] In some countries, such as Chile, private debt is a much larger fraction of the total, raising special problems in cases of debt rescheduling (section 4).

The nearly fivefold rise in debt from 1973 to 1982 (table 1) represented average annual growth of 19 percent. However, after deducting for inflation, the real debt of nonoil developing countries has risen only by a multiple of 2.1 over the last decade, indicating real growth of 8.7 percent annually— still a rapid rate but one of less startling dimensions. Considering that real growth of GDP has averaged 4.5 percent in 1973–82 for nonoil developing countries,[9] the weight of external debt relative to domestic production has

8. World Bank, *World Debt Tables,* 1982–83 ed. p. viii.

9. IMF, *World Economic Outlook,* 1982, p. 144 and 1983, p. 171.

1978	1979	1980	1981	1982
336.3	396.9	474.0	550.0	612.4
286.6	338.1	388.5	452.8	499.6
281.0	294.7	308.6	331.3	357.8
258.3	333.0	419.8	444.4	427.4
130.2	119.2	121.9	124.9	143.3
19.0	19.0	17.6	20.4	23.9
11.0	6.9	4.9	11.7	22.3
28.5	27.5	27.6	31.0	34.7
13.9	16.2	20.4	21.0	19.9

risen in the last decade (from 22 percent of GDP in 1973 to 35 percent in 1982, table 1). Nonetheless, because developing countries have achieved export growth that is more rapid than GDP growth, the ratio of external debt to exports of goods and services has risen by considerably less, from 115 percent in 1973 to 143 percent in 1982 (table 1).

The reassurance provided by growing exports is less convincing when the debt-service burden, as opposed to debt itself, is taken into account. Primarily because of rising interest rates, debt service (interest on short- and long-term debt plus amortization on long-term debt) has risen from an average of 15.4 percent of exports of goods and services in 1973–77 to 18.5 percent in 1978–80 and 22.2 percent in 1981–82.

To be sure, some of this increase in the debt-service ratio, at least until 1980, was attributable to a higher inflationary component of interest rates. Higher inflation tends to cause higher interest rates. When this occurs, higher current debt service must be paid—because approximately two-thirds of developing-country debt is at floating interest rates tied to the London Interbank Offer Rate (LIBOR).[10] But higher inflation also erodes the real value of the debt that eventually is to be repaid. Accordingly, high interest rates caused primarily by high inflation have the effect of causing a greater present cash flow burden in return for eroding the real value of outstanding debt. In effect, they cause accelerated amortization of the debt in real terms.

This process of inflationary acceleration of debt repayment through higher nominal interest rates was important through most of the 1970s. As shown in table 1, the adjusted "real debt-service ratio" deducting the inflationary erosion of principal was considerably lower than the nominal debt-service ratio through much of the period.[11] By 1981–82, however, nominal interest rates were high while inflation was declining. As a result, the adjusted "real" debt-service ratio rose in 1981 to a higher level (11.7 percent) than in any previous year for a decade, and it then proceeded nearly to double (to 22.3 percent) in 1982 as inflation fell sharply while interest rates fell more slowly.

Another disconcerting trend in the external debt is the rising share of short-term debt (original maturity less than one year) in the total. Short-term debt rose from 8.7 percent of the total in 1973 to 14.6 percent in 1974–79 and 18.1 percent in 1980–82 (table 1), showing a rise to a new plateau after each oil shock. The susceptibility of short-term debt to sudden disruption in normal renewal, once creditor confidence erodes, makes its rising share a source of instability. And short-term borrowing is an especially unreliable form of financing for long-term development. Ideally, loan maturities should match those of investment projects.

The broad pattern shown in table 1 is that although developing-country debt grew rapidly in the 1970s this growth was much more moderate when judged in real terms and relative to the export base. However, by 1981 the burden of debt rose significantly on all three principal measures—ratio of debt to exports, real (adjusted) debt-service ratio, and ratio of debt to GDP. And in 1982 these measures of debt burden rose still further, to levels (in each case) not previously experienced. As can be seen in table 1, an important cause of the sharp deterioration in 1982 was an actual decline in the nominal value of exports (by 3.8 percent) even as total debt continued to rise (by

---

10. See section 3.

11. For calculation of the adjusted real debt-service ratio, total debt-service payments are reduced by the amount of US wholesale price inflation in the year in question as applied to outstanding debt at the end of the previous year.

10.3 percent). Export stagnation was driven both by global recession (which caused export volume growth to decline) and by dollar appreciation and commodity price erosion (lowering the dollar value of export earnings). As discussed below, domestic policies in debtor countries also played a role in increasing debt in important cases. In sum, the underlying data on developing-country debt confirm that significant economic erosion in 1982 lay behind the emergence of acute debt-servicing difficulties in several countries, including the most important debtor nations.

The pattern shown in table 1 provides useful aggregate background, but debt difficulties occur at the level of individual countries. Accordingly, table B-1 of the statistical appendix presents data on debt trends individually for the 10 developing and East European countries with the largest external debt. As that table shows, for certain key debtor countries debt trends have shown a greater increase in debt burden than is apparent in the aggregate data just examined. Thus, for the three largest debtors, debt growth has been far greater than the fivefold (nominal) multiple for all developing countries (1973–82). For Brazil the rise has been a multiple of 6.4, to $88 billion; for Mexico, a multiple of 9.5 to $82 billion; and for Argentina, a multiple of 5.9, to $38 billion. The debt-service ratio has risen far more dramatically for these leading debtors than for developing countries on average. Compared with a rise from 16 percent in 1973–74 to approximately 24 percent by 1982 for all developing countries, Brazil's debt-service ratio rose from 36 percent to 87 percent, Mexico's from 25 percent to 58 percent, and Argentina's from 21 percent to 103 percent (appendix table B-1). Moreover, although these countries' relative debt burdens gradually increased through the 1970s, there was an especially sharp rise in 1982. Thus, the ratio of net debt (debt *minus* foreign reserves) to exports of goods and services rose from 257 percent in 1981 to 365 percent in 1982 in Brazil, from 209 percent to 249 percent in Mexico, and from 275 percent to 354 percent in Argentina.

The data for individual countries also reveal important cases where the debt burden has been kept at a relatively low level. Thus, Korea had a ratio of net debt to exports of only 104 percent in 1982; Indonesia, 86 percent; and Venezuela (because large reserves offset much of its debt), 104 percent— all well below the average for developing countries.[12] In short, the debt trends for individual developing countries tend to confirm erosion in 1982 in

---

12. Additional country detail is included in William R. Cline, *International Debt: Systemic Risk and Policy Response* (Washington: Institute for International Economics, forthcoming 1983), hereafter referred to as *International Debt*.

TABLE 2 **Export growth[a] compared with interest rates, 1973–82**
(percentage)

	1973	1974	1975	1976	1977
LIBOR + 1 percent	10.2	12.0	8.0	6.6	7.0
Export growth, nominal					
Nonoil LDCs	n.a.	36.4	1.4	16.5	21.2
Net oil importers	n.a.	33.1	1.6	16.3	21.9
Net oil exporters	n.a.	57.3	−0.1	18.9	18.8
Brazil	56.1	33.2	6.1	13.5	19.7
Mexico	26.8	31.6	−0.2	13.3	14.0
Argentina	61.6	25.8	−23.9	30.8	43.6
Korea	85.6	29.4	9.7	60.8	38.2
Venezuela	54.4	126.8	−15.7	2.8	5.5
Chile	49.0	60.1	−21.7	31.7	8.1

n.a. Not available.
Source: International Financial Statistics, selected issues, IMF *World Economic Outlook,* 1983, and Institute for International Economics debt data base.
a. Goods and services.

particular but, in addition, a more serious extent of the underlying problem in certain countries (especially in Latin America) where temporary debt-servicing breakdowns have in fact occurred within the last year.

Mario Henrique Simonsen, former planning minister of Brazil, has proposed a useful summary criterion to determine whether a country's debt-servicing burden is improving or getting worse.[13] Simonsen's criterion is that export earnings must be growing at a higher rate than the interest rate. Otherwise, the country's debt burden tends to worsen. The logic of this rule of thumb is that there is an automatic "inherited" increase in debt by the amount of past debt multiplied by the interest rate, because this amount is the interest due on past debt. If the country is achieving a balanced foreign account (current account) excluding interest, then its debt will grow by this amount. That is, its debt will grow by the interest rate. If the ratio of debt to exports is to avoid increasing (maintaining a constant relative debt burden), exports

13. Mario Henrique Simonsen, "The Financial Crisis in Latin America" (Rio de Janeiro: Getúlio Vargas Foundation, 1983; processed).

1978	1979	1980	1981	1982
9.7	13.0	15.4	17.5	14.1
17.2	28.9	26.1	5.8	− 3.8
16.9	26.8	24.2	5.4	− 3.8
18.0	40.4	35.4	7.8	− 3.6
7.2	24.2	29.3	15.7	− 13.4
39.1	40.2	54.3	21.9	7.3
16.3	26.6	13.0	5.1	− 15.7
31.3	13.8	15.6	21.7	2.3
− 0.8	50.2	36.4	10.1	− 22.0
13.8	59.0	32.2	− 2.6	− 3.8

must also grow by at least this rate. As a consequence, exports should grow at a rate no less than the interest rate.[14]

The sea change in debt-servicing viability in 1981–82 may be seen by examining this summary criterion. In table 2, a typical interest rate on developing-country loans—LIBOR plus a spread of 1 percent—is compared to the nominal export growth rate for 1973–82. Until 1980 the interest rate averaged 10.2 percent, while the growth rate of exports for nonoil developing countries averaged 21.1 percent. The interest rate test was clearly being met and overfulfilled. But in 1981–82, the interest rate averaged 15.8 percent, while export growth in these countries averaged only 1.0 percent. The actual decline of exports in 1982 was especially damaging. A sharp change had occurred, with higher interest rates conflicting with slower export growth, and the condition for avoiding deterioration in the relative debt burden was

---

14. This rule no longer applies when the country is running a trade surplus and transferring net resources abroad rather than receiving them. In that case the debt does not automatically grow at the interest rate, and export growth may be more modest. However, under normal conditions developing countries receive net resource inflows rather than transferring net resources abroad.

no longer being met. The table also shows export growth for individual major debtors. The declines in average export growth were severe for most of the countries listed that did experience debt-servicing difficulty in 1982–83 (Argentina, Brazil, Chile, Mexico, Venezuela).

The table also shows that once before in the past decade, in 1975, the condition comparing export growth to the interest rate was also violated. In that year the global recession caused slow export growth. However, unlike the 1981–82 period, there was no widespread incidence of debt-servicing disruption in 1975. The difference between the interest and export-growth rates was smaller (6.6 percent in 1975 compared with an average of 14.8 percent in 1981–82), reflecting the fact that the 1975 recession was shorter and less severe. Moreover, the relative severity of the debt burden was milder going into the 1975 recession (as measured by debt relative to exports and GDP, and the debt-service ratio, table 1).

In sum, various measures of relative debt burden show a sharp erosion in 1981–82 as well as (by at least some criteria) milder earlier erosion in the 1970s, both in the aggregate and for key individual debtor countries. The principal causes of the eroding debt situation include both global influences and domestic policies of the debtor country. The global, or external causes of the debt problem include higher oil prices in 1973–74 and 1979–80, high international interest rates—especially in 1981–82, and global recession in 1980–82—which not only reduced the growth of export volume for developing countries but also caused a sharp deterioration in their terms of trade. Domestic policies included crucial decisions on exchange rates, domestic budgetary policy, and growth strategy generally. In addition, there is the question of the role of possibly overly accommodative foreign private banks, an issue considered in section 5.

Oil Prices

The single most important exogenous cause of the debt burden of nonoil developing countries is the sharp rise in the price of oil in 1973–74 and again in 1979–80. As shown in table 1, the value of oil imports rose from 6 percent of total merchandise imports in 1973 to 20 percent in 1980–82. Table 3 presents a simple calculation of the cumulative additional costs of oil imports imposed on the net oil-importing developing countries by these price rises. The first column shows actual net oil imports by these countries since 1973. The second column shows the amount that would have been paid for these imports if the price of oil had risen no more than the US wholesale price

TABLE 3   **Impact of higher oil prices on debt of nonoil developing countries**[a]
(billion dollars)

| | Oil imports | | Additional cost |
Year	Actual (A)	Hypothetical (B)[b]	(C = A − B)
1973	4.8	4.8	0.0
1974	16.1	5.3	10.8
1975	17.3	5.7	11.6
1976	21.3	6.8	14.5
1977	23.8	7.5	16.3
1978	26.0	8.6	17.4
1979	39.0	10.9	28.1
1980	63.2	11.9	51.3
1981	66.7	12.1	54.6
1982	66.7	11.9	54.8
Total, 1974–82	344.9	85.5	259.5

Source: IMF, *World Economic Outlook*, 1982, p. 163, and *International Financial Statistics*, selected issues.
a. Net oil importers only.
b. If oil prices had risen no more than US wholesale price index from 1973.

index after 1973.[15] (Note that by 1973 oil prices had already risen by 42 percent from their 1972 level.) As the table shows, the cumulative total of the additional expense on oil imports amounts to $260 billion over the decade. This amount includes no allowance for cumulative interest charges on each year's additional oil bill, which would make the additional debt even larger. On the other hand, the estimates do not refer to actual increase in debt but potential increases before taking account of offsetting factors, especially adjustment measures adopted to reduce nonoil imports and increase exports, and increased exports to OPEC countries.

It is reasonable to ask whether oil-exporting developing countries achieved corresponding export gains that made their debt lower than it would have been. Among the countries grouped as "nonoil developing countries" by international practice,[16] only Mexico is now a major exporter of oil. Yet

15. This value *equals* column A *times* the ratio of the US wholesale price index to the index of oil prices (Saudi Arabia), with both indexes set at 100 for 1973.

16. See, for example, International Monetary Fund, *World Economic Outlook*, 1983.

Mexico's large build-up of debt was almost certainly accelerated rather than deterred by higher oil prices. Mexico first borrowed heavily to develop oil production, and subsequently the promise of oil exports was the main basis for its ability to borrow large amounts more generally in pursuit of a high-growth strategy. Among the other oil-exporting developing countries, it is difficult to argue that the debts of Venezuela, Nigeria, Indonesia, and Ecuador are substantially lower than they would have been in the absence of higher oil prices (with the possible exception of Venezuela if debt net of reserves is considered); indeed, the ratio of their 1982 debt to the 1973 level is higher than for the nonoil developing countries. Accordingly, the net impact of higher oil prices was an unambiguous increase in developing-country debt of extremely large dimensions.

It does not follow from this analysis that the problem of world financial vulnerability to external debt would be relieved by a collapse in the price of oil. On the contrary, by now the oil-exporting developing countries (including Mexico) have built up large debt, and the adverse impact of a sharp drop in the price of oil would be highly concentrated for them while the corresponding benefits for oil-importing developing countries would be more modest (because oil is a much smaller fraction of their imports than it is of oil exporters' earnings from exports). As is often the case in economic (or physical and political) phenomena, the sharp increase of oil prices carried with it certain irreversibilities, including financial strains for the system as a whole that could not now be eliminated by the sudden return of oil prices to their 1973 levels. The issue of the impact on debt of lower oil prices is examined in section 3. The main thrust of the preceding analysis is that a legacy of the 1970s is a high level of debt attributable to an international force exogenous to the debtor countries: the sharp rise in the price of oil.

Interest Rates and Recession

If higher oil prices set the stage for a heavy debt burden for many countries in the last decade, the global recession and high interest rates of 1980–82 added sufficiently to the burden to precipitate several major debt crises by 1982.

Borrowers became accustomed to low real interest rates in the 1970s. For 1961–70, LIBOR on US dollar deposits *minus* the US wholesale price increase produced an average real interest rate of 4.1 percent. But for 1971–80, this average was −0.8 percent: real interest rates were negative on average for the decade.[17] By 1979 and 1980 nominal interest rates were high (LIBOR averaged 13.2 percent) and although (US) inflation was virtually equal to LIBOR, high nominal rates caused a cash-flow squeeze for borrowers as discussed above. By 1981–82 declining inflation without a corresponding decline in interest rates meant high real interest rates (7.5 percent in 1981 and 11.0 percent in 1982), making matters worse.

Because of higher interest rates, caused largely by the unusual mix of monetary and fiscal policy adopted in the United States in 1981–82, the average interest rate on outstanding long-term debt of developing countries rose from 4.5 percent in 1973–77 to 8.5 percent in 1981–82[18]; deducting (US) inflation the real interest rate on this debt rose from −6 percent to +3 percent over the same period.

To obtain a notional magnitude of the increase in debt attributable to higher interest rates, it is possible to estimate the "excess interest rate" in 1981–82 as the amount by which real interest rates exceeded their average level for 1961–80. For the 1960s and 1970s real interest rates (LIBOR *minus* US wholesale price inflation) average 1.66 percent. In 1981 this real rate was 7.46 percent, and in 1982 it reached 10.95 percent.[19] Thus, the excess of interest rates above the real level that might have been expected based on the past two decades was 5.8 percentage points in 1981 and 9.29 percentage points in 1982.

Approximately two-thirds of developing-country debt is indexed to LIBOR (section 3). Deducting nongold reserves (most of which earn interest), the nonoil developing countries had net floating debt of $240 billion at the end of 1980 and $293 billion at the end of 1981 (rising to $329 billion at the end of 1982). Applying the estimated excess interest costs in 1981 and 1982 to the year-end debts of 1980 and 1981, respectively, total excess interest payments on developing-country debt amounted to $41 billion in 1981–82, beyond amounts developing-country borrowers could have anticipated on the basis of past real interest rates. The basic cause of this excessive interest rate was the mismatch between loose fiscal policy and tight monetary policy in

---

17. IMF *International Financial Statistics Yearbook*, 1982.

18. IMF *World Economic Outlook*, 1982, p. 173. For funds borrowed commercially at a typical rate of LIBOR plus 1 percent spread, the corresponding rise was from 8.8 percent to 16.8 percent, in nominal terms, and from −1.6 percent to 11.3 percent in real terms.

19. IMF *International Financial Statistics*, various issues.

the United States, which drove up domestic (and therefore international) interest rates in textbook fashion.

Coinciding with and in considerable degree because of, high real interest rates, the international economy experienced severe recession in 1980–82. From 1973 to 1979 real growth in industrial countries averaged 3.2 percent annually. It then fell to 1.2 percent in 1980–81 and −0.3 percent in 1982.[20] Commodity export prices for developing countries are sensitive to the business cycle, and by 1981–82 they showed substantial declines. With 1980 = 100, export unit values fell to an index of 94 in 1981 and 90 for 1982 in nonoil developing countries. Import unit values rose to 103 in 1981 and returned to 100 by 1982.[21] Applying these changes to the trade bases (goods and services) of the previous year (table 1) the resulting effects were a loss of $25 billion in export value and an import cost increase of $9.6 billion in 1981, and a loss of export value in 1982 by $44 billion but no increment in import costs (compared with 1980 prices). Thus, the total loss to nonoil developing countries from deteriorating terms of trade in 1981–82 was an estimated $79 billion.

Real export volume also stagnated as the result of a 1980–82 world recession. Real export growth for nonoil developing countries averaged 8.1 percent in 1971–80.[22] Real export growth was 9.9 percent in 1981 and only 1.8 percent in 1982, giving an average shortfall for the two years that, when applied to the base of exports of goods and services, implies a net loss of $21 billion from trend in real exports.

In sum, high interest rates and the global recession imposed large cumulative losses on the nonoil developing countries in 1981–82. In all, these countries lost approximately $141 billion in higher interest payments, lower export receipts, and higher import costs as the consequence of adverse international macroeconomic conditions.

The (ex ante) impact of all of these exogenous shocks on external debt of the nonoil developing countries is summarized in table 4. As the table shows, their combined impact (on an ex ante, or potential, basis) was to increase the debt of nonoil developing countries by $401 billion. The table also shows

20. IMF *World Economic Outlook*, 1983.

21. IMF *International Financial Statistics*, May 1983, pp. 56–57.

22. Calculated from IMF *International Financial Statistics Yearbook*, 1982, using export values as deflated by unit values of exports.

TABLE 4   **Impact of exogenous shocks on external debt of nonoil developing countries**
(billion dollars)

Effect	Amount
Oil price increase in excess of US inflation, 1974–82 cumulative[a]	260
Real interest rate in excess of 1961–80 average: 1981 and 1982	41
Terms-of-trade loss, 1981–82	79
Export volume loss caused by world recession, 1981–82	21
Total	401
Memorandum items	
Total debt: 1973	130
1982	612
Increase: 1973–82	482

Source: Author's calculations; see text.
a. Net oil importers only.

the total increase in external debt of these countries since 1973, amounting to $482 billion.

By their nature these estimates are not strictly comparable to actual debt increases after the fact, because countries did pursue adjustment measures to reduce external deficits (and debt) from levels they otherwise would have reached. Thus, in Korea higher oil prices in 1979–81 raised the cost of oil imports from $2.2 billion in 1978 to $6.1 billion in 1982. But because of strong measures to adjust by raising exports, Korea's trade balance actually improved, from a deficit of $1.3 billion in 1978 to one of $0.8 billion in 1982.[23] Accordingly, it would not be proper to conclude from table 4 that 83 percent of increased debt ($401 billion/$482 billion) was caused by these exogenous shocks—other influences not measured here could well have contributed considerably more (ex ante) than the remainder of $81 billion, and the final debt build-up was substantially smaller than the sum of all such ex ante influences (because of adjustment). Nonetheless, these figures strongly suggest that a very large part of the increase in developing-country debt in the last decade may be attributed to the impact of global causes that were exogenous to the developing countries themselves: higher oil prices beginning

23. IMF *International Financial Statistics,* various issues.

in 1973 and, in 1981–82, abnormally high interest rates and declines in terms of trade and export volume associated with global recession.

Domestic Policies

In addition to serious outside shocks from the world economy, domestic policy errors contributed to the deterioration of the debt situation. In Mexico, the government allowed the peso to become seriously overvalued, and allowed budget deficits to surge to 16.5 percent of GNP in 1982 when the upcoming presidential election made authorities reluctant to carry out effective budget-cutting measures. The government adhered to a strategy of high growth (8.2 percent annual growth in 1978–81) that probably exceeded capacity growth and failed to take adequate account of the substantial weakening of the oil market in 1981.[24]

In Brazil, domestic adjustment policies were stronger and indeed contributed to a severe recession that began in 1981 and continued into 1983. Even so, Brazil's domestic policies bear substantial responsibility for the eventual crisis in 1982. Throughout the 1970s after the first oil shock, Brazil consciously followed a high-risk strategy of pursuing high growth based on rapid accumulation of external debt. The resulting legacy of large debt proved to be an oppressive burden when the international economy weakened and exports declined instead of continuing their earlier rapid growth.[25] Matters were made worse by overvaluation of the cruzeiro after an ill-fated attempt to bring down domestic inflation by placing a 40 percent ceiling on devaluation in 1980. Nonetheless, by 1981 the government was taking adjustment measures and was typically considered by the international financial community to be managing the economy well.

In Argentina a policy of preannouncing an exchange rate devaluation by less than the rate of domestic inflation, in an attempt to bring down inflation, led to a vastly overvalued peso, high imports, poor export performance, and rapidly rising debt by 1981. Ineffective stabilization policy, collapse of the

24. William R. Cline, "Mexico's Crisis, The World's Peril," *Foreign Policy,* no. 49 (Winter 1982–83), pp. 107–18.

25. William R. Cline, "Brazil's Aggressive Response to External Shock," in William R. Cline and Associates, *World Inflation and the Developing Countries* (Washington: Brookings Institution, 1981), pp. 102–35.

peso, and extremely high inflation in 1981 were followed by the adverse shock to credit markets from the Falklands war and the associated mutual freeze of assets between the United Kingdom and Argentina. In Chile, much more stringent monetary and fiscal policy led to success in bringing down inflation in the 1970s (in contrast to Argentina's failure to do so). Nonetheless, a similar conceptual approach to reducing inflation by preannouncing the exchange rate led to a similar problem of overvaluation of the peso, which, together with a decline in the price of copper, led to rapid increase in debt. In Venezuela, lax management of state agencies permitted build-up of short-term debt after 1976 despite the presence of surpluses in the external accounts and large external assets in the petroleum agency. In Poland, foreign borrowing to avoid domestic economic restraint, and the domestic political clash between the Solidarity trade union and the government, led to increased debt, a severe decline in economic activity, lower exports, and exhaustion of reserves.

In Venezuela and Mexico especially, but also in other cases to some extent, policies led to large capital flight abroad. The basic flaw was maintenance of an overvalued exchange rate on a fully convertible basis, combined with domestic interest rate policy that failed to provide sufficient attraction to retain capital domestically. As a consequence, in 1982 the decline in Venezuela's official external assets reached over $8 billion, although on current account its deficit was only $2.2 billion.[26] Similarly, in Mexico errors and omissions showed outflows of $8.4 billion in 1981 and $6.6 billion in 1982 and short-term capital outflows added $2.1 billion in 1982, for total capital flight of $17 billion.[27] In Argentina, in 1980 and 1981 errors and omissions and short-term capital outflows registered total capital flight of $11.2 billion.[28] Thus, recent capital flight has contributed nearly one-third of total debt in both Venezuela and Argentina, and approximately one-fifth in Mexico. This fact not only raises the issue of the quality of the economic growth and capital formation purchased by higher debt in these particular countries, but it also raises questions about the advisability of international official financing of such capital flight through the mounting of support packages to put new public and private money into the country from

26. UN Economic Commission for Latin America, *Preliminary Balance of the Latin American Economy in 1982* (Santiago, January 1983), p. 13.

27. Banco de Mexico, *Informe Anual* (Mexico City, 1982), p. 230.

28. IMF *International Financial Statistics*, May 1983, p. 68.

abroad even when national citizens are removing their own assets from the country. At the least it implies the need for strong domestic measures (realistic exchange and interest rate policies) to prevent future substantial capital flight.

In addition to short-term policy errors such as those just enumerated, there have been long-run development strategies that have been less than ideal. Excessive protection in programs of industrialization based on import substitution, inadequate pricing of capital, over-pricing of labor, overly ambitious and inefficient government enterprise activities, and other distortions have hindered efficient development in many developing countries.[29] The cyclical pressures from the global economy have made it more essential that distortions in basic development strategies be corrected.

This review of policy mishaps does not mean that the bulk of developing-country borrowing has been unproductively used. Aside from the notable amounts of capital flight in the three Latin American countries cited above, the use of most borrowing appears to have been productive. Thus, domestic savings did not decline in the 1970s when external financing was heavy. For middle-income oil-importing countries, gross domestic savings were 21 percent of GDP in 1980 compared with 19 percent in 1960, and gross domestic investment was 27 percent compared with 21 percent,[30] suggesting that not only did foreign financing help increase domestic investment, but also that it was not used for the purpose of raising domestic consumption and reducing domestic savings.[31] Similarly, for 10 major borrowing developing countries, the average savings rate rose from 20.6 percent of GNP in 1965–73 to 21.9 percent in 1974–79, and the investment rate rose from 20.4 percent to 22.6 percent.[32]

---

29. See World Bank, *World Development Report 1983*, Part II (Washington, 1983).

30. World Bank, *World Development Report 1982* (Washington, 1982), p. 118.

31. Note that this judgment is not contradictory to the analysis that higher oil expenditure contributed to the debt. The bulk of oil use in developing countries tends to be as an intermediate input into production (for example, in truck transportation) rather than for consumption (in pleasure driving, for example). Accordingly, it is not appropriate to view oil imports primarily as consumption, and as inelastic response of these imports to higher price as a failure to carry out necessary reductions in consumption.

32. Jeffrey D. Sachs, "The Current Account and Macroeconomic Adjustment in the 1970s," *Brookings Paper on Economic Activity*, no. 1 (Washington: Brookings Institution, 1981), pp. 201–68.

It must also be recognized that by the late 1970s, a large part of new net borrowing was going merely to pay the interest on past debt (section 4, table 19). In evaluating the productive or unproductive use of borrowing, it is first necessary to deduct this portion, as a given cost of the borrowing process. The central question is whether the remainder of net borrowing went primarily to capital formation or into consumption, capital flight, and other less productive uses such as military purchases. The available econometric analysis of developing-country borrowing has tended to find that it was associated with acceleration of productive investment rather than used primarily for consumption purposes.[33]

In sum, there have been significant domestic as well as foreign causes of the debt problem. This conclusion has also been found in various detailed studies of the causes of debt-servicing difficulties.[34] Nonetheless, it would be inaccurate to conclude that the bulk of the debt contracted has failed to go into productive investments; the evidence tends to indicate that most borrowing was productively used. But it remains true that because the magnitudes of the external economic pressures on developing countries became so great (especially by 1981–82), as examined above, there was little margin left for domestic policy error. In evaluating domestic policy, it must also be kept in mind that the sharp decline in the global economy, rise in interest rates, and oil price shock of 1980–82 were generally not predicted, and few would have advocated the extremely cautious borrowing policy that would have been consistent with foreknowledge of these global shocks.

Psychology

International debt problems have been aggravated by psychological shifts in the credit markets. In both Eastern Europe and Latin America, a debt-servicing breakdown by a major country has led relatively rapidly to a process of regional contamination that has severely restricted capital flows to most of the rest of the region. Poland's quasi-default in 1981 demonstrated that the "umbrella" theory of Soviet backing for East European debt was invalid,

---

33. *Ibid.*

34. See in particular Stanley W. Black, "The Impact of Changes in the World Economy on Stabilization Policies in the 1970s," in *Economic Stabilization in Developing Countries,* ed. William R. Cline and Sidney Weintraub (Washington: Brookings Institution, 1981), pp. 43–77.

and credit quickly became scarce for the region, pushing Romania into rescheduling and placing pressure on other governments in the region. Thus, the net exposure of Western banks in Eastern Europe declined from $46 billion in 1980 to $42 billion by mid-1982.[35]

The Mexican debt crisis of August 1982, added to the Argentinian disruption of debt servicing associated with the Falklands war, caused a similar adverse shock to credit supply for Latin America as a region. In September of 1982 lending to Brazil fell to half its monthly average for earlier in the year.[36] By mid-1983 problems of credit availability and resulting debt rescheduling in Latin America had spread to Brazil, Chile, Peru, and Venezuela, and previous debt-servicing difficulties (and reschedulings) persisted in Costa Rica, Nicaragua, Bolivia, and Ecuador. The only significant exception to regionwide debt-servicing disruption was Colombia, a country that had carefully avoided incurring heavy debt (at the recognized cost of less buoyant growth) and had placed the receipts of the late-1970s' coffee bonanza into reserves instead of using them as leverage for further borrowing. The abrupt curtailment of credit to Latin America was evident in the data for US bank loans outstanding, which rose from $68.1 billion in June 1982 to $69.3 billion in December, an increase of only $1.2 billion compared with $7.3 billion in the same period during 1981.[37]

To be sure, there was also underlying deterioration in the debt-servicing capacity of many of the Latin American countries in 1982, largely because of the depressed level of their exports (which fell from $97 billion in 1981 to $87 billion in 1982 for the region as a whole).[38] Nonetheless, the sharp psychological shift aggravated debt problems and at least in some cases (especially Peru) probably precipitated debt-servicing disruptions that otherwise could have been avoided.[39]

---

35. BIS, *The Maturity Distribution of International Bank Lending* (Basle), selected issues.

36. William R. Cline, "Mexico's Crisis."

37. Federal Financial Institutions Examination Council, *Country Exposure Lending Survey* (Washington), various issues. The figures cited exclude countries in the region that are members of OPEC.

38. UN Economic Commission for Latin America, "Preliminary Balance," p. 13.

39. See the analysis in "A Logit Model of Debt Rescheduling, 1967–82," in *International Debt*.

Summary

The external debt crisis that emerged in many developing countries in 1982 can be traced to higher oil prices in 1973–74 and 1979–80, high interest rates in 1980–82, declining export prices and volumes associated with global recession 1981–82, problems of domestic economic management, and an adverse psychological shift in the credit markets. External debt of developing countries has grown to large dimensions, and in 1981–82 that growth outpaced the growth of exports that sustain the debt. Because of the magnitude of this debt and the widespread, if not generalized, evidence of debt-servicing difficulties, the debt problem currently poses a considerable risk to the security of the international financial system.

2   System Vulnerability and Emergency Response

The international financial system is vulnerable to the potential impact of default or serious disruption in the servicing of the debt of developing and East European countries. This vulnerability stems largely from the fact that much of the debt is owed to private banks in industrial countries, and the amounts owed are large relative to bank capital. Because banks play a pivotal role in national economies, and because their loans are highly leveraged on a relatively small capital base, loss of a significant part of their capital from developing-country defaults could place severe strains on the Western economies.

The events of September 1982 through mid-1983 demonstrated graphically that Western policymakers acknowledge the vital importance of the viability of the external debt of several large debtor nations to the international financial system. As temporary debt-servicing breakdowns emerged in or threatened major debtors, the international financial community reacted promptly with financial rescue packages. This section first examines the extent of the system's vulnerability to external debt, and then reviews the emergency measures taken and their prospects for success.

Bank Exposure

Significant default on sovereign debt last occurred in the 1930s. But most of the debt was in the form of bonds. While its loss hurt individual bondholders, the damage did not extend beyond them. Today the bulk of sovereign debt to private sources is in the form of bank lending. Because banks are highly leveraged financial intermediaries, the economic damage from default could be multiplied severalfold.

The risk to banks from foreign lending may be gauged by examining the size of their exposure to the class of foreign borrowers most likely to encounter debt-servicing difficulties: developing and East European countries. The exposure in these countries may be compared to the banks' capital base. For US banks, table 5 shows the ratio of exposure to capital since 1977 when

TABLE 5 **Exposure of US banks in Eastern Europe and nonoil developing countries, relative to capital**

(percentages, end year)

	1977	1978	1979	1980	1981	1982	Value, 1982 (million dollars)
All banks							
Eastern Europe	16.7	15.8	16.1	13.9	12.9	8.9	6,278
Nonoil LDCs	114.9	114.4	124.2	132.3	148.3	146.1	103,181
Sum	131.6	130.2	140.3	146.2	163.5	155.0	109,459
Mexico	27.4	23.4	23.0	27.6	34.3	34.5	24,377
Brazil	29.4	28.6	27.3	25.4	26.9	28.9	20,438
Nine largest banks							
Eastern Europe	25.0	23.5	23.9	21.8	19.5	13.9	4,045
Nonoil LDCs	163.2	166.8	182.1	199.3	220.6	221.2	64,149
Sum	188.2	190.3	206.0	221.1	240.1	235.2	68,194
Mexico	32.9	30.4	29.6	37.8	44.4	44.4	12,262
Brazil	41.9	42.4	40.3	39.3	40.8	45.8	13,296

Source: Federal Reserve Board of Governors, *Country Exposure Lending Survey.*

the country exposure reporting system began. It is evident from this table that the exposure of US banks in nonoil developing and East European countries is high. For all banks this exposure has risen from 131.6 percent of capital in 1977 to 155 percent in 1982. If five OPEC countries not in capital surplus are included (Algeria, Ecuador, Indonesia, Nigeria, Venezuela) the 1982 total exposure stands at 182.8 percent of capital. For the nine largest banks relative exposure is even higher: 235.2 percent of capital for East European and nonoil developing countries and 282.8 percent including the five OPEC countries just cited.

The trends in table 5 highlight the pullback from Eastern Europe since the Polish debt disruption of 1981. By 1982 exposure in Eastern Europe had fallen to slightly over half its size relative to capital in the late 1970s. The table also documents the sharp rise in loans to Mexico: for the nine largest banks, an increase from 30 percent of capital in 1978–79 to 44 percent by 1982, with a similar rise for all banks. The paramount role of Mexico and Brazil is shown in the table: each accounts for about one-third of the capital of all banks and about 45 percent of the capital of the nine largest banks. Together Mexico and Brazil represent 35 percent of total US bank loans to Eastern Europe, nonoil developing countries, and five OPEC countries.

It should be kept in mind that although exposure to these countries is high relative to bank capital, it is a more modest share of total bank loans. Thus, for the nine largest banks, loans to the set of countries considered here (including five OPEC countries) account for 282.8 percent of capital but only 13.9 percent of total bank assets (primarily, loans). The difference between the two concepts stems from the high leverage of banks, whose loans are as much as twenty times as large as their capital.

The exposures of individual large banks to individual countries potentially in debt-servicing difficulty provide a more direct reflection of vulnerability. Table 6 shows the exposure of 18 large individual banks to five Latin American countries that have all experienced debt-servicing difficulties (of varying degrees) in the last year. The exposure is expressed as a percentage of primary capital (the same capital measure as that used in table 5). From the table it is evident that certain key banks have considerably greater exposure relative to capital than might be expected based on more aggregate data. Exposure in Brazil is approximately three-fourths of the capital of Citicorp and Manufacturers Hanover; exposure in Mexico equals or exceeds 60 percent of capital for Manufacturers Hanover, Chemical Bank, and First Interstate. Exposure in these five Latin American countries alone exceeds 150 percent of capital for Citicorp, BankAmerica, Chase Manhattan, Manufacturers Hanover, Chemical, and Crocker National.

In short, for the US banking system as a whole and for some of the largest US banks in particular, exposure to developing countries poses a substantial

TABLE 6 **Exposure as percentage of capital, major banks, end-1982**

	Argentina	Brazil	Mexico	Venezuela	Chile	Total	Capital[a] (million dollars)
Citibank	18.2	73.5	54.6	18.2	10.0	174.5	5,989
Bank of America	10.2	47.9	52.1	41.7	6.3	158.2	4,799
Chase Manhattan	21.3	56.9	40.0	24.0	11.8	154.0	4,221
Morgan Guaranty	24.4	54.3	34.8	17.5	9.7	140.7	3,107
Manufacturers Hanover	47.5	77.7	66.7	42.4	28.4	262.8	2,592
Chemical	14.9	52.0	60.0	28.0	14.8	169.7	2,499
Continental Illinois	17.8	22.9	32.4	21.6	12.8	107.5	2,143
Bankers Trust	13.2	46.2	46.2	25.1	10.6	141.2	1,895
First National Chicago	14.5	40.6	50.1	17.4	11.6	134.2	1,725
Security Pacific	10.4	29.1	31.2	4.5	7.4	82.5	1,684
Wells Fargo	8.3	40.7	51.0	20.4	6.2	126.6	1,201
Crocker National	38.1	57.3	51.2	22.8	26.5	196.0	1,151
First Interstate	6.9	43.9	63.0	18.5	3.7	136.0	1,080
Marine Midland	n.a.	47.8	28.3	29.2	n.a.	n.a.	1,074
Mellon	n.a.	35.3	41.1	17.6	n.a.	n.a.	1,024
Irving Trust	21.6	38.7	34.1	50.2	n.a.	n.a.	996
First National Boston	n.a.	23.1	28.1	n.a.	n.a.	n.a.	800
Interfirst Dallas	5.1	10.2	30.1	1.3	2.5	49.2	787

n.a. Not available.
Source: Annual reports for individual banks; *American Banker,* 17 March 1983 and 6 April 1983; Prudential-Bache Securities, ''Banking Industry Outlook,'' May 6, 1983; *Veja* (Brazil), 1 June 1983. Capital figures are from reports of condition (Federal Reserve).
a. Bank capital includes shareholders equity, subordinated notes, and reserves against possible loan losses.

potential vulnerability. Nonetheless, it is necessary to have a general idea of the extent to which this broad class of external debt stands at risk. One simple basis for examining this question is to examine the debt totals for the class of countries that have indeed experienced significant debt-servicing interruptions within the last year. In several cases these include new or former debt reschedulings. In most of the cases (perhaps with the notable exception of Poland), the reschedulings should provide the basis for adequate future meeting of debt commitments, albeit with subsequent reschedulings in certain cases. Recognizing, then, that such a listing tends to overstate the pool of potentially risky loans, the data in table 7 present total bank lending (US and

TABLE 7 **Debt owed to industrial-country[a] banks by developing and East European countries, June 1982**

	Debt (billion dollars)	Debt service[b] as percentage of exports of goods and services (1982)	Debt servicing disruption in 1982–83
Mexico	64.4	58.5	yes
Brazil	55.3	87.1	yes
Venezuela	27.2	20.7	yes
Argentina	25.3	102.9	yes
South Korea	20.0	21.1	no
Poland	13.8	n.a.	yes
Chile	11.8	60.4	yes
Philippines	11.4	36.1	no
Yugoslavia	10.0	30.3	yes
East Germany	9.4	29.0	no
Algeria	7.7	41.0	no
Hungary	6.4	33.0	no
Indonesia	8.2	11.3	no
Nigeria	6.7	5.4[e]	no
Taiwan	6.4	n.a.	no
Israel	6.1	23.7	no
Colombia	5.5	23.9[e]	no
Egypt	5.4	39.0	no
Malaysia	5.3	5.0[e]	no
Peru	5.2	53.4	yes
Subtotal	311.5		
Of which			
Debt disruption	213.0		
Total, LDCs[c] and Eastern Europe[d]	374.9		

Source: Bank for International Settlements, *The Maturity Structure of International Bank Lending*, Basle, December 1982; Institute for International Economics debt data bank; and Wharton Econometric Forecasting Associates (GDR, Hungary).
a. Group of Ten plus Switzerland, Austria, Denmark, and Ireland.
b. Excluding short-term principal, including short-term interest.
c. Including Yugoslavia; excluding Middle Eastern capital-surplus oil-exporting countries.
d. Excluding USSR.
e. 1981.

other industrial countries) to the 20 countries with the largest debt owed to banks, and the table indicates whether the country experienced debt-servicing interruption in 1982–83 (and reports the ratio of its debt service to exports of goods and services). Perhaps the most severe case of disruption is that of Poland; the least severe (primarily management difficulties in shifting short-term to long-term debt), Venezuela. Using this definition, however, and considering that smaller countries not singled out in the table are having comparable difficulties, fully two-thirds of the bank debt owed by Eastern Europe and developing countries was under a cloud of interruption in normal debt servicing in 1982–83.

The thrust of the preceding analysis is that not only does bank exposure to Eastern Europe, nonoil developing countries, and noncapital-surplus OPEC countries reach nearly 300 percent of capital for the nine largest US banks and nearly 200 percent for all US banks, but approximately two-thirds of this debt is in some sense at risk as revealed by interruption in debt servicing in 1982–83. Accordingly, potential vulnerability of the financial system must be taken seriously.

Even under the worst of circumstances, however, this body of debt would be unlikely to become worthless overnight. Indeed, in the vast majority of rescheduling cases the debt is carried at book value and, at least until further evidence of protracted failure to meet rescheduled payments legitimately, can continue to be carried at full value on the banks' books.

Moratorium Consequences

The stages of debt-servicing difficulty beyond rescheduling include "extended moratorium" whereby no principal or interest is paid for a period of, perhaps, more than six months, and outright "repudiation." In the last quarter century only Cuba and North Korea have repudiated external debt. As discussed in section 4, the costs of repudiation for a country are likely to be so high that this alternative is rarely chosen. A country in severe straits is more likely to announce that it can make no payments for a considerable period of time.

For Western banks, repudiation of a substantial portion of loans to developing countries and Eastern Europe would be crippling. Even widespread moratoria could have a severe impact on the banks. To gauge the potential risk, it is useful to consider how far international debt would have to deteriorate to cause banks to pass beyond certain thresholds of deterioration themselves.

A first threshold is the level of bank profits. Foreign loan losses would in the first instance be set against profits before affecting capital. In 1982 gross profits (before tax) of the nine largest US banks amounted to $5.5 billion.[40] Their total loans to nonoil developing countries, Eastern Europe, and five noncapital-surplus OPEC countries stood at $82 billion at the end of 1982, or 15 times as large as gross profits.

Regulatory practice on provisioning (setting aside of reserves) on doubtful loans has been to require that up to 50 percent be provisioned over a five-year period. On average, approximately 10 percent of the principal would be set aside in each year, and 15 percent yearly thereafter (although these patterns are not rigid and depend on individual bank decisions). With annual gross profits of $5.5 billion, the nine largest banks could afford to provision only 30 percent of their loans to developing and East European countries out of annual profits.[41]

Nor would there appear to be much relief from the standpoint of offsetting tax effects. Although financial institutions can carry back losses for 10 years and thereby obtain tax refunds, US banks in practice have paid little tax in the past—only 2.7 percent on domestic income for the 20 largest banks in 1981.[42] Accordingly, there would be little in past tax payments to use as a recoverable offset against new losses from external lending.

As a similar, but perhaps even more hypothetical, illustration, consider what would happen if Argentina, Mexico, and Brazil were to miss one year's payment on principal and interest, and were to do so in a sufficiently aggressive way that it seemed appropriate to write off fully the payments missed. The complete loss of one year's payments due from these three countries would cause losses equal to 28 percent of the capital of the nine

---

40. Paine, Webber, Mitchell, Hutchins, Inc., "Earnings Models for Large US Banks," *Status Report* (June 14, 1983).

41. Let x be the amount of developing-country loans that must be provisioned and y the amount of gross bank income. Assuming interest of 12 percent on these loans, $.12x$ would be forgone income as the payments are missed, reducing gross income to $y - .12x$. Maximum provisioning out of profits is then $.10x = y - .12x$, or $x = 4.5y$. Considering that total developing-country and East European debt is 15 times gross bank profits, only 30 percent of these loans (4.5/15) could be provisioned out of profits. This calculation assumes that missed interest payments would not be counted in profits (i.e., using accrual accounting). Otherwise, there would be little if any "real" provisioning (because such phantom payments would probably exceed the 10 percent yearly provisioning rate), and the bank would find itself having made no effective allowance at all for principal loss.

42. *Internal Revenue Code,* section 172 (New York: The Research Institute of America, Inc., 1980), pp. 160–61; *Washington Post,* 10 March 1983.

largest US banks even after taking account of offsetting profits on other loans.[43]

Based on these two illustrations, situations could arise (although with a low degree of probability) in which losses from Third World debt could cut heavily into the capital of Western banks. To pursue the illustration of a write-off of one year's payments from Argentina, Brazil, and Mexico, although the resulting cut in capital would not cause insolvency, it would mean that the banks would have to begin to reduce their total loans sharply in order to reestablish the 5 percent ratio of capital to loans required by regulators.[44] There would thus be a multiple reduction in loans. Potentially the nine largest banks would have to cut their loans outstanding by approximately $160 billion as the result of a loss of $8 billion of their capital from one year's loss of principal and interest from Argentina, Brazil, and Mexico under conditions where these losses had to be written off. Both because of loan cutbacks and because of a sharp increase in the risk premium, the interest rate could be expected to rise, causing recessionary pressure. Even if the Federal Reserve loosened the capital backing of loans temporarily, the potential would exist for economic shock waves through reduced credit availability to American business and consumers and, as a result, increased unemployment.

To a considerable extent, the sequence of events that would follow major bank losses because of country losses remains uncharted waters. The process just described of loan reduction by affected banks seeking to reestablish their capital-to-loan ratios would be clearly contractionary. However, to the extent that central banks made loans to the affected private banks in an attempt to replace at least partially the repayments that otherwise would have been received from countries failing to make payments, there could be inflationary consequences. When a country makes loan payments to bank A, it tends to

---

43. These three countries owe $31.3 billion to the nine largest banks, whose capital broadly defined is only $29 billion. Together the three countries owe the nine largest banks approximately $3.4 billion in interest, $6.9 billion in short-term debt payments, and $3.4 billion in long-term debt payments for 1983, before recent restructurings. The total owed is $13.7 billion for 1983. By contrast, 1982 profits of these banks were $5.5 billion before taxes. Thus a loss of $13.7 billion would cause total losses of $8.2 billion or 28 percent of capital and, without offsetting items generating taxes, these losses would have to be fully absorbed out of capital.

44. Although the capital requirement for large banks has not been rigid, it is becoming more so as regulators respond to increasing congressional pressure. A new formal requirement of 5 percent capital backing for large banks was adopted in mid-1983. *Wall Street Journal,* 10 and 20 June 1983.

do so using funds newly borrowed from bank B or else funds drawn from its account of export earnings held at bank B. The withdrawal at one bank tends to offset the repayment to the other, leaving little net monetary effect on the banking system as a whole. But if, in place of the country's payment, the central bank (Federal Reserve, in the case of the United States) makes a loan of comparable size to the private bank, there can be a net expansion of the monetary base, permitting an expansion of the money supply by a multiplied amount for the banking system as a whole. Essentially, a payment from the home country's central bank is an injection of high-powered money that serves as the basis for multiplied monetary expansion. However, the Fed could use other measures (open market sales of Treasury bills, for example) to offset the inflationary injection of these loans, unless it decided that crisis circumstances warranted faster monetary expansion.

In practice some combination of these measures would probably occur in a debt crisis. In addition, the regulatory agencies could permit reduced capital-to-loan ratios; Congress might provide mechanisms to inject public capital if capital ratios fell below a minimal level (as in the case of recent legislation for a safety net for thrift institutions); and write-offs could be spread over a number of years. And the central banks could perhaps gauge the amount of their lending so that the inflationary effect of injection of high-powered money just offset the contractionary effect of bank-loan cutbacks designed to restore capital-to-loan ratios.

Despite the fact that the Federal Reserve could respond in a crisis, there would be enormous economic risks from a large-scale banking crisis. If a wider front of country defaults were to occur, many major banks could become insolvent. For the nine largest banks this result would occur if just Brazil, Mexico, and Argentina repudiated their debt, or if all developing and East European countries experienced sufficient difficulty that one-third of their debt had to be written off. Normally bank insolvencies are dealt with by merger, with a larger, sound bank absorbing the bankrupt concern. But in the situations just described, merger would be highly unlikely. There would be no banks larger than the failing banks to absorb them. In the past merger has tended to guarantee the deposits of all depositors. In a bankruptcy of the major banks, however, it is likely that only deposits covered by the Federal Depositors' Insurance Corporation (FDIC) would be guaranteed (in the United States), a maximum of $100,000 per account. For the US banking system, deposit insurance covers only 73 percent of total deposit value.[45]

---

45. According to information supplied by the FDIC.

By central banking principle, the central bank supports illiquid banks but not insolvent ones. Accordingly, a truly massive failure of external debt could bring down many major banks. Regardless of the emergency public measures that might be mounted in response, the potential economic consequences could be devastating. Accordingly, those (including some in Congress and the financial press) who advocate policies that would ignore this risk (for example, opposition to adequate resources for the International Monetary Fund) should be recognized as high-stake gamblers.

In sum, because developing and East European country exposure is so large relative to bank capital, any large-scale write-down of this debt would have dramatic effects on the banks, cutting deeply into their capital and exerting pressure for them to reduce the level and growth of their lending. Potentially serious domestic economic disruptions could result, with possible contractionary as well as inflationary consequences, and with large possible losses for the considerable portion of deposits not covered by insurance. For these reasons most policymakers take the problem of Third World debt very seriously indeed.

Rescue Operations, 1982–83

In view of the potential damage to the international financial system from a collapse of the debt of developing countries, especially that of the largest debtors, the decisive response of US and other Western officials to the major debt crises of 1982 was reassuring. There were four major rescue operations: for Mexico, Brazil, Argentina, and Yugoslavia. The International Monetary Fund played a major role in all four. US authorities took the lead in the packages for Mexico and Brazil, while the Swiss did so in the case of Yugoslavia. The basic model of the rescue packages included country adjustment, an IMF program, bank lending, and official bridging loans.

Argentina's debt problem lingered over several months as arrears built up after the Falklands crisis. But when Mexico suspended principal payments in mid-August 1982, the stakes were clearly so large that foreign official response was immediate. The United States quickly mobilized $1 billion in commodity credits and $1 billion in prepayment for oil purchases for the strategic oil reserve, and it led a lending package from Western central banks through the Bank for International Settlements (BIS). The loans from central banks were short-term, designed to provide a bridge to expected IMF lending. Private banks agreed to an initial delay in principal payments and subsequently to major rescheduling and provision of new loans. By November Mexico had signed an agreement with the IMF.

In the case of Brazil rapid erosion in capital market confidence led to a large emergency loan from the United States in November 1982 and to recourse to IMF borrowing—a step the government had sought to avoid. An IMF agreement was reached rapidly, and by year's end a rescue operation similar to Mexico's was broadly in place. Argentina's package progressed much more slowly but an IMF agreement was finally signed early in 1983. For its part, Yugoslavia developed payments problems at the end of 1982 as it found itself unable to borrow the required amounts from banks. By early 1983 Western governments, banks, and international lending institutions had put together a $6 billion credit package for Yugoslavia, in a form that avoided outright debt rescheduling.[46]

In managing these rescue packages, the International Monetary Fund adopted a new approach of historical significance. Contrary to previous practice, whereby the IMF merely hoped that an adoption of a stand-by lending program would act as a seal of approval to encourage the return of foreign private lending, the IMF now explicitly told the private banks that if they did not provide new lending themselves there would be no new IMF funds whatsoever. In a situation in which many banks sought to withdraw, this strategy gave them no alternative but to bear their fair share in extending new loans. This approach was an effective answer to the ''free-rider'' problem (section 4), whereby especially the smaller banks seek to enjoy the benefits of increased quality of their exposure from provision of new international lending by large banks without providing any new lending themselves.

The elements of the international rescue packages for Argentina, Brazil, Mexico, and Yugoslavia are shown in table 8. Some key elements of the packages were more limited than they appeared because of their very short-term nature: loans from the BIS, the US Treasury, and the Federal Reserve. These loans had to be repaid typically within 90 days, meaning that they added nothing to the cash flow for 1983 as a whole and served solely as bridging loans until the IMF and bank packages could be assembled. Similarly, the amounts from the IMF and from the banks are not comparable, because the IMF amounts (except for Argentina) were the full amount that could be expected over the next three years (at least in the absence of an extraordinary decision to exceed 450 percent of quota, or new quota increases without reduced percentage-of-quota access), while new bank lending was just for

---

46. *Washington Post,* 21 January 1983.

TABLE 8 **Financial rescue packages for Argentina, Brazil, Mexico, and Yugoslavia**
(billion dollars)

	Argentina	Brazil	Mexico	Yugoslavia
Financial support				
IMF				
Stand-by	1.7	—	—	0.6
Extended Fund facility	—	4.6	3.7	—
Compensatory finance and other	0.5	1.3	0.22	—
World Bank	—	—	—	0.3
Bank for International Settlements	0.5	1.2	0.925	0.5
United States				
Oil payments	—	—	1.0	—
Commodity Credit	—	—	1.0	0.2
Federal Reserve	—	0.4	0.925	—
Treasury	—	1.53	—	—
Private banks, new loans	1.5	4.4	5.0	3.8[b]
Government trade credits	—	—	2.0	1.1
Total	4.25	13.4	14.7	6.5
Debt rescheduling				
Amount	5.5	4.9	19.5	n.a.
Originally due	1982–83	long-term 1983	8/1982 to 12/1984	n.a.
Coverage	public	public	public	n.a.
Pending negotiation	all private[a]	n.a.	15.0 private	n.a.

— Zero or negligible.

n.a. Not applicable.

Source: House of Commons, Treasury and Civil Service Committee, *International Monetary Arrangements International Lending by Banks* (London, 15 March 1983), pp. xxviii–xxix; *Wall Street Journal,* 9 May 1983.

a. Pressure on banks to maintain short-term credit lines.

b. New loans, $600 million; $1.4 billion to repay matured debt; $1.8 billion stretch-out of short-term loans.

1983 and additional new bank lending could be expected again in 1984 and 1985, ideally on a voluntary basis but perhaps again on an involuntary basis. Given these nuances, the table shows massive international support in these rescue operations.

Debt rescheduling was a central part of these packages (except in Yugoslavia, where loan rollovers were used to avoid the stigma of rescheduling). Once again, just as the IMF informed banks that it expected new money, it also informed them that the IMF funding would be forthcoming only if the banks committed themselves to reschedule certain portions of debt coming due. Typically rescheduling was on a five-to-eight year basis, involved rescheduling fees (from ½ percent for Mexico to 1½ percent for Brazil), and carried relatively high interest rate spreads (typically about 2 points over LIBOR or US prime). In Mexico, all public debt due in 1982 after August and through 1984 was rescheduled. This amount reached approximately $20 billion, much of which was short term. In Argentina, arrears on short- and long-term private debt had reached $2.8 billion by early 1983, and all public debt in arrears as well as that due in 1983 was rescheduled. In Brazil, only the public long-term debt due in 1983 was rescheduled, because Brazil made an extreme effort to distance itself from being classed as a standard rescheduling case—for fear of injury to its credit standing in the longer run. Instead, Brazil secured commitments of banks to maintain the levels of their short-term exposures, obviating outright rescheduling of short-term debt but setting the stage for subsequent problems as these bank commitments were not fully met (in the component for interbank deposits in foreign branches of Brazilian banks).

By mid-1983 the principal rescue packages appeared to be functioning relatively well.[47] Argentina and Mexico were meeting their policy commitments under the IMF agreements, and both had relatively good prospects of achieving their external current account goals for the year—although primarily at the cost of severe domestic recession as the mechanism for reducing imports in the case of Mexico.

In Brazil, however, the program was preceding less smoothly. Failure to meet internal targets (such as that for reducing the budget deficit) meant that the IMF suspended its support until additional measures and new targets could be agreed upon. A central problem was that a large devaluation in February 1983 had boosted inflation, thereby making targets established in

47. See John Williamson, ed., *Prospects for Adjustment in Argentina, Brazil, and Mexico: Responding to the Debt Crisis* (Washington: Institute for International Economics, June 1983).

specific monetary amounts much tighter than originally planned, in real terms. Moreover, of the four-part bank package established for Brazil, the part concerning interbank deposits was failing to meet the target level (only $6 billion was being maintained compared with $7.5 billion planned). As a result, Brazil had built up nearly $900 million in arrears by mid-year.[48] Ironically, prospects looked relatively good for meeting the external current account target; it was the weakness of the initial financial plan that was causing the immediate difficulty.

Broadly, however, the rescue packages of 1982–83 met the immediate challenge of risk to the international financial system. By mid-1983, the central policy question concerned not so much the feasibility of immediate financial rescue (even the Brazilian problems seemed likely to be manageable after limitation of domestic wage indexing paved the way for reinstatement of the IMF package, although there was a considerable likelihood that some new measures would be required to mobilize an additional $3 billion or more in foreign credit even within 1983). Rather, the issue increasingly was whether over the medium term the debt problems could be managed as tractable liquidity problems, or whether instead the prospects for debt servicing were so bleak that public policy should be radically revised to treat the debt problem as one of insolvency, using methods analogous to bankruptcy proceedings. The answer to this question depends not only on the domestic political tolerance for adjustment measures but also on the likely international economic environment over the medium term.

3   Debt Prospects, 1983–86

The severity of the problem of international debt may be judged best by a close examination of the likely developments in balance of payments and external debt of the principal debtor countries in the medium term. Only such an analysis, rather than recourse to general arguments or extrapolation of past trends, can provide a concrete evaluation of whether systemic risk from international debt is likely to abate or intensify. The analysis requires projections at the level of individual major countries, because treatment of

---

48. *Financial Times*, 31 May 1983.

aggregates tends to mask emerging problems of specific countries. This section develops a computer-based projection model that incorporates the influence of varying global economic conditions as well as alternative adjustment efforts by the debtor countries themselves.

Insolvency or Illiquidity?

In debt problems of domestic firms, there exists a classic distinction between a firm that has positive net worth but is illiquid and one that simply has negative net worth, and is therefore insolvent. The most fundamental policy issue today concerning international debt is whether the major debtor countries are illiquid or insolvent: whether their obligations should be viewed as largely sound debt or bad debt. If they are merely illiquid, additional lending is appropriate to tide them over short-term difficulties. If they are insolvent, it may be more appropriate to recognize their debt as bad debt and to attempt to salvage at least some portion of the debt while accepting some loss on face value, analogously to domestic bankruptcy proceedings whereby creditors attempt to secure so many cents on the dollar. The proliferating proposals for write-offs and stretchouts (section 7) typically adopt the implicit view that the problem is insolvency, not illiquidity.

To analyze whether the problem of developing-country debt is one of insolvency or illiquidity, it is necessary to examine the prospective path of the balance of payments and debt of the major debtor countries over the medium term. The concept here is the "potential" or "ex ante" balance of payments, given at least minimally acceptable growth rates in the debtor countries. If the prospective external deficits are so large that there is no plausible way they can be financed taking into account the severely shocked state of international credit markets, then the diagnosis must be one of insolvency. However, if instead the projected deficits are of a size that is consistent with reasonable magnitudes of financing, and especially if the prospective deficits relative to exports (and other indicators of debt-servicing difficulty) show an improving trend, then the appropriate diagnosis is one of illiquidity.

The conceptual distinction between illiquidity and insolvency is less clear-cut for a country than for a firm. Unlike firms, countries do not disappear. However, they can reach a point of inability to service debt over an extended time period, thereby becoming much like bankrupt firms from the standpoint of creditors. When applied to countries, the categories of illiquidity and insolvency should be seen as metaphorical rather than absolute. Accordingly, the distinction between the two should be recognized as a broad framework for policy analysis, rather than a uniquely defined classification that can be measured precisely. In particular, the basic approach of the quantitative analysis presented here is to examine whether trends are toward improvement or deterioration. It must remain to some extent ambiguous as to whether projected improvement is sufficient for a clear verdict of illiquidity or projected deterioration so severe as to constitute outright insolvency.

A Projection Model

The approach of this study is to conduct alternative projections of balance of payments and debt for the 19 largest debtor countries for the period 1983–86.[49] These countries account for approximately two-thirds of the total external debt of developing and East European countries, and for three-fourths of the debt of this set of countries owed to private banks.[50] The analysis is conducted at the level of the individual country, considering that group aggregates tend to disguise the severity of debt difficulties that may arise in individual countries.

The strategy of the model is to calculate the external current account deficit, other balance of payments items, and external debt for each country

---

49. The full exposition of this model appears in William R. Cline, *International Debt.*

50. The totals here include nonoil developing countries, Eastern Europe, and the following OPEC countries: Ecuador, Indonesia, Nigeria, and Venezuela. The 19 countries examined here, by size of total debt, are: Brazil, Mexico, Argentina, Korea, Venezuela, the Philippines, Indonesia, Israel, Turkey, Yugoslavia, Chile, Egypt, Algeria, Portugal, Peru, Thailand, Romania, Hungary, and Ecuador. Because of inadequate data for analysis, Poland (with external hard currency debt of approximately $24 billion at the end of 1982) is omitted from the analysis. For private banks reporting to the Bank for International Settlements, the total owed to banks by Latin America, Asia, Africa, Eastern Europe excluding the Soviet Union, and the Middle East (excluding Iran, Iraq, Kuwait, Libya, Qatar, Saudia Arabia, and the United Arab Emirates as capital-surplus OPEC countries) amounted to $379.3 billion in June 1982. The corresponding total for the 19 countries examined here was $291.1 billion. Bank for International Settlements, "The Maturity Distribution of International Bank Lending" (Basle, December 1982). For total debt (including short-term), the 19 countries have aggregate debt of $484.2 billion (end-1982), compared with a total for the broad set of countries described above amounting to $739 billion. Calculated from International Monetary Fund, *World Economic Outlook,* 1983, p. 200, for nonoil developing countries ($612 billion); *Wall Street Journal,* 8 April 1983, for East European ($53 billion); and the estimates of this study for Algeria, Indonesia, Venezuela, and Ecuador.

for each year through 1986 under alternative assumptions about world economic conditions. These alternatives are specified in four areas: the rate of economic growth in industrial countries, the international interest rate (LIBOR), the price of oil, and the real exchange rate of the dollar relative to other major currencies. In addition, the model is driven by assumed internal actions of the developing countries: their growth rates and their exchange rate policy. These influences, domestic and internal, determine the course of individual items in the balance of payments year by year, beginning with actual data for 1982 balance of payments.

The model specification is as follows. For oil-exporting countries, the value of oil exports equals the value in the base year (1982) multiplied by the ratio of the international price of oil in the year in question to the 1982 price, or $34 per barrel. (Note that this approach makes no allowance for change in volume of oil exports.) Similarly, for oil-importing countries, the value of oil imports equals their value in the base year times the ratio of price in the year in question to price in the base year.

Nonoil exports depend on the rate of growth in industrial countries and on the real exchange rate adopted by the country. The influence of industrial-country growth is twofold: it affects the volume growth of exports as well as their terms of trade. Based on statistical estimates in an earlier study, it is assumed that above a threshold of OECD growth at 1 percent per year (where developing-country export growth is zero) each extra percentage point of OECD growth causes an additional growth of 3 percent in the volume of developing-country exports.[51]

In addition, the model captures the response of real export prices (terms of trade) to industrial-country growth. Commodity prices are sensitive to the business cycle so that, when industrial-country growth is high, developing-country exports of commodities tend to experience larger price increases than average world inflation; and when the trough of the cycle arrives, these commodity prices tend to fall by more than the decline, if any, in general world prices. In the model here, "real" nonoil export prices for the country in question increase by a given percentage amount (typically 3) for each percentage point change in industrial-country growth. (This formulation

---

51. William R. Cline and C. Fred Bergsten, "Trade Policy in the 1980s: An Overview of the Problem," in *Trade Policy in the 1980s*, ed. William R. Cline (Washington: Institute for International Economics, forthcoming 1983). The formulation here is: $g_m = -3 + 3g_{dc}$, where g_m is percentage growth of OECD imports from developing countries, and g_{dc} is OECD growth rate. The constant term -3 is larger than in the original estimate (-4.6) to account for higher trend growth of developing-country exports to the OECD than total OECD import growth.

means that once a stable growth rate plateau is reached there is no further change in terms of trade). The response of terms of trade to OECD growth varies by country and is based on statistical estimates for 1961–81.

The next element in calculating export value is a factor for world inflation. The value of exports increases along with the average rate of world inflation (in national currencies, of major industrial countries) in the year in question. There is also a similar inflator for the effect of dollar depreciation on the dollar price of goods in world trade. Experience in recent years has shown that when the dollar appreciates (or depreciates) relative to other major currencies by a given percentage, the dollar price of exports from industrial countries (a measure of world trade prices) tends to decline (rise) by a similar percentage from the rate of inflation that otherwise would be expected from OECD inflation.[52] This term is important because if the dollar depreciates from its currently high level, the effect will be a rise in the dollar value of developing-country exports (as they parallel world trade prices) and a recuperation of the nominal level of these exports relative to the largely dollar-denominated external debt.

The remaining elements in the calculation of future exports capture the effect of the country's own real exchange rate on its exports (the amount of domestic currency, for example, pesos, per dollar, deflating both pesos and dollars by home-country and US prices, respectively). Thus, a real depreciation causes the country's exports to rise by one-half percentage point for each percentage point of real depreciation. (This impact is spread over two years.) In sum, nonoil exports are driven by OECD growth, world inflation, dollar strength, and the country's real exchange rate. Total exports *equal* nonoil *plus* oil exports.

The forces influencing nonoil imports are domestic economic growth in the developing country in question, world inflation and dollar devaluation, and the real exchange rate. Nonoil imports grow by a percentage reflecting the long-term growth relationship between real imports and real GDP, assumed to be a one-for-one relationship (1 percent trend growth in GDP

---

52. Thus, in 1979–80 exports of industrial countries rose in dollar price by an average of 14.1 percent; the number of special drawing rights (SDRs) per dollar changed by an average of −1.9 percent (dollar depreciation); and average OECD inflation was 11.4 percent. In 1981–82, industrial-country exports had an average dollar price change of −3.2 percent; SDRs per dollar changed by an average of 8.6 percent (dollar appreciation); and OECD inflation averaged 9.0 percent. Using the simple relationship, dollar export inflation *equals* OECD inflation *minus* dollar appreciation, these figures conform relatively well to the expected relationship, especially in 1979–80.

causes 1 percent import growth). In addition, there is a shorter run cyclical response of imports to income that is typically greater than the long-run trend response (because of factors such as inventory adjustments and temporary protection). It is assumed that a short-run cyclical increase of GDP by 1 percent increases imports 3 percent.

Like exports, imports rise in dollar value in response to additional world inflation and dollar depreciation. Furthermore, a change in the country's real exchange rate by 1 percent causes 0.6 percent change in the country's imports (spread over two years, as in the case of exports). Thus, the country can adjust by depreciating its real exchange rate to reduce imports. Total imports *equal* oil *plus* nonoil imports.

The parameters chosen to indicate the responsiveness of exports and imports to real exchange rate changes ("trade elasticities") are selected to be consistent with past empirical evidence and to strike a balance between "elasticity pessimism" and "optimism," both of which may be found in the international trade literature. Turning to other elements of the balance of payments, exports and imports of nonfactor services (transportation, freight and insurance, tourism) are calculated, respectively, as constant proportions of nonoil exports and imports, determined from base-year levels. Imports of services are defined to include net profits remittances.

Interest payments are calculated as follows. The fraction of long-term debt that is at fixed interest rates, and the average interest rate paid on fixed interest debt in 1982, are determined. For all remaining external debt—short- and long-term—it is assumed that the interest rate paid equals the international rate (LIBOR) plus a spread of 1½ percent (or, for Brazil, 2 percent). Interest earnings on nongold reserves are assumed to be earned at a US Treasury bill rate assumed to equal 1½ percentage points below LIBOR. Net interest payments are thus the fixed interest rate *times* the portion of debt at fixed rates, *plus* the variable interest rate *times* the portion of debt at variable rates (including short-term), *minus* the interest earnings on reserves. For these calculations, debt and reserves at the end of the preceding year are applied.

As a final element of the current account, private transfers are estimated on the basis of simple 3 percent real growth as inflated by the path of dollar depreciation. The current account balance is then the sum of the above elements: exports of goods and services *minus* imports of goods and services, *minus* interest payments, *plus* transfers.

Given the current account, the capital account is constructed as follows. The change in reserves is assumed to equal either zero, if imports decline, or one-fifth of the rise in imports if they rise—to maintain an acceptable reserve cushion relative to imports. Direct foreign investment is assumed to grow at a real rate of 3 percent annually, as inflated for dollar depreciation. The total amount of new net lending required to finance the balance of payments then *equals* the current account deficit *plus* the rise in reserves, *minus* the amount of direct foreign investment. Total debt at the end of the year *equals* the previous year's debt *plus* net borrowing, and the composition of debt between short- and long-term is assumed to remain the same as in the base period. Amortization on long-term debt *equals* the country's base period amortization rate (ratio of long-term debt amortization to end-of-year long-term debt in the previous year), applied to long-term debt at the end of the preceding year. Gross borrowing *equals* net borrowing *plus* amortization.

To evaluate trends in debt-servicing burden and creditworthiness, four ratios are calculated: the ratio of debt service to exports of goods and services (DSR); the ratio of net debt to exports of goods and services (NDX); the ratio of the current account balance to exports of goods and services (CAX); and the ratio of reserves to imports of goods and services, excluding interest (RSM). Data used in the model are described in Appendix A.

The following values are assumed for the basic model simulations. For developing-country growth, it is assumed that real GDP grows by 2½ percent in 1983, 3½ percent in 1984, and 4½ percent in 1985 and 1986. The 1983 rate reflects zero per capita growth on average, and even the 4½ percent rate for 1985–86 is well below the average of the past decade. Moreover, both Brazil and Mexico are assumed to experience − 2 percent in growth in 1983. For country exchange rates, it is assumed that all of the major debtors devalue in real terms by 5 percent in 1983 and by 3 percent in 1984. As exceptions, Mexico is assumed to devalue by 5 percent in 1983 but not thereafter (because the sharp curtailment of imports by restrictions and exchange control in 1982 meant the base year already reflected the potential impact of large devaluation). For Brazil real devaluation is set at 15 percent, for Argentina 10 percent, and for Chile 17 percent, in 1983, given large recent devaluations in these countries.

The basic simulations of the model assume the alternative parameters specified in table 9. Given the alternative values in each of the four dimensions (industrial-country growth, price of oil, LIBOR, and dollar devaluation), a total of 40 combinations results. The basic set of inflation assumptions is applied to all variants. It assumes moderate inflation of 5 percent per year, 1983–86. The base-case assumptions were verified as mutually consistent on the basis of the world economic model of Data Resources, Inc. As shown in this table, the base case assumes a 3 percent rate of OECD growth in

TABLE 9 **Alternative global economic parameters**

	1982	1983	1984	1985	1986
Industrial-country growth (percentage)					
A	0.0	1.0	1.5	1.5	1.5
B	0.0	1.5	2.0	2.0	2.0
C	0.0	1.5	2.5	2.5	2.5
D*	0.0	1.5	3.0	3.0	3.0
E	0.0	2.0	3.5	3.5	3.5
Oil price (dollars/barrel)					
A*	34.0	29.0	29.0	29.0	34.0
B	34.0	20.0	20.0	25.0	25.0
LIBOR (percentage)					
A*	15	10	9	8	8
B	15	11	13	15	15
Dollar (index)					
A*	1.00	1.05	1.15	1.15	1.15
B	1.00	1.00	1.05	1.05	1.05
Inflation (percentage)	4	5	5	5	5

* Base-case assumption.

1984–86. Although this assumption might seem optimistic, it must be kept in mind that recovery from severe world recession would normally yield growth rates considerably higher. Indeed, in order for 1981–86 growth to equal the average OECD growth rate for 1971–80 (3.2 percent), it would be necessary for 1984–86 growth to average 5.7 percent, considering the low growth of 1981–83. Notably, the International Monetary Fund anticipates 3 percent real growth in the 1984.[53] With respect to the other base-case assumptions, the abnormally high current level of the dollar warrants an assumed depreciation of 15 percent over two years; pressure in US capital markets from large budget deficits indicates that although interest rates may decline they are unlikely to fall very far; and on oil prices, some leaders of OPEC itself are now predicting no change in the official price of $29 per barrel through 1985. The alternative hypotheses provide for even sharper decline in the price of oil (in view of the market's weakness for the past two

53. IMF *World Economic Outlook*, 1983, p. 4.

years), higher interest rates (in light of US budget deficits), and less depreciation of the dollar (considering safe-haven effects and the possibility of higher interest rates).

Results

The results of the basic simulations show three central conclusions. First, under the base case for growth of the world economy (1½ percent in 1983, 3 percent annually in 1984–86), the severity of the debt problem recedes substantially. Second, the problem is responsive to global growth: if growth is 2½ percent or below, the situation remains little improved or deteriorates. Third, there is a strong tendency for the debt situation to improve for the oil-importing countries but to become more severe for the oil-exporting countries.

The full results of the simulations are presented in a forthcoming volume.[54] For purposes of final analysis, however, the basic results include specific country adjustments, to account for the fact that in the initial estimation of the model with the uniform country assumptions outlined above, a number of countries showed highly favorable trends in current account balances (Brazil, Korea, Turkey, Romania) while others show such large deficits that their financing is implausible (Algeria, Venezuela, Chile). Accordingly, domestic growth rates are increased or devaluations reduced in the first group, while growth rates are reduced and the real exchange rate depreciated further in the second group, to reflect additional scope for growth or need for greater adjustment.[55] The reductions in growth from the standard assumption are sharpest for Venezuela and Algeria; in view of their past exceptional gains from higher oil prices, below-average growth in the 1980s would seem politically feasible.

Table 10 presents the aggregate results of the base case (where industrial-country growth is 1½ percent in 1983 and 3 percent thereafter), with

---

54. William R. Cline, *International Debt*.

55. The following adjustments are made to the internal policies of these countries, beyond any unique assumptions in the base case. (1) For Korea, Turkey, and Romania, 6 percent growth is assumed for 1983–86, and there is no devaluation. (2) For Brazil, 6 percent growth is assumed for 1984–86. (3) For Venezuela and Algeria, devaluation of 7 percent is assumed in 1983 with another 7 percent in 1984, and growth is set at −2 percent in 1983 and only 2 percent in 1984–86. (4) For Chile, growth is set at zero in 1983, 2 percent in 1984, 3 percent in 1985, and 4 percent in 1986.

TABLE 10 **Projections of balance of payments and debt, base case, 1982–86**
(million dollars and ratios)

	1982	1983	1984	1985	1986
Oil importers					
Exports	110,536	125,243	158,805	179,936	199,758
Imports	− 125,552	− 135,360	− 159,308	− 174,566	− 194,848
(oil)	− 34,499	− 29,426	− 29,426	− 29,426	− 34,499
Interest	− 29,464	− 29,256	− 30,058	− 29,591	− 30,187
Current account	− 35,451	− 30,890	− 20,207	− 12,564	− 12,626
Debt	299,377	327,595	346,638	355,816	365,535
Net debt/exports	1.94	1.88	1.55	1.40	1.28
Debt service/exports	0.39	0.38	0.32	0.28	0.26
Oil exporters					
Exports	76,300	69,783	74,836	78,072	89,813
(oil)	59,140	50,443	50,445	50,443	59,140
Imports	− 64,756	− 66,835	− 84,013	− 92,747	− 101,070
Interest	− 15,423	− 16,520	− 16,886	− 18,305	− 21,284
Current account	− 20,989	− 19,711	− 33,973	− 40,933	− 40,674
Debt	184,778	201,558	234,702	272,769	310,119
Net debt/exports	1.77	2.04	2.13	2.35	2.36
Debt service/exports	0.34	0.40	0.38	0.40	0.41
Total, 19 countries					
Exports	186,836	195,026	233,642	258,008	289,571
Imports	− 190,308	− 202,195	− 243,321	− 267,314	− 295,918
Interest	− 44,887	− 45,775	− 46,944	− 47,896	− 51,471
Current account	− 56,440	− 50,602	− 54,181	− 53,498	− 53,300
Debt	484,155	529,153	581,340	628,585	675,654
Net debt/exports	1.87	1.94	1.74	1.70	1.62
Debt service/exports	0.37	0.38	0.34	0.32	0.30

Source: Author's calculations.

groupings into oil-importing and oil-exporting countries and with the adjustments just described for 7 individual countries. For the 19 countries combined, the current account deficit declines from $56 billion in 1982 to $53 billion in 1986. In real terms at 1982 prices (adjusting for world inflation—but not

TABLE 11 **Current account and debt projections: major debtors, 1982–86**[a]
(million dollars and ratios; base case)

		1982	1983	1984	1985	1986
Brazil	CA	−14,000	−7,131	−4,729	−1,041	−647
	D	88,200	93,060	95,843	94,231	92,347
	NDX	3.816	3.463	2.642	2.244	1.965
Mexico	CA	−4,254	−2,321	−5,899	−6,970	−6,005
	D	82,000	82,619	87,573	92,877	96,957
	NDX	2.727	2.817	2.582	2.526	2.316
Argentina	CA	−2,400	−2,476	−825	257	996
	D	38,000	39,752	39,583	38,175	35,898
	NDX	3.720	3.383	2.572	2.146	1.796
Korea	CA	−2,219	−1,720	−334	628	664
	D	35,800	37,826	38,860	38,599	38,524
	NDX	1.060	0.999	0.827	0.725	0.635
Venezuela	CA	−2,200	−4,363	−9,021	−10,681	−10,615
	D	31,800	35,537	45,075	55,781	66,473
	NDX	1.042	1.438	1.910	2.474	2.639

CA current account; D total debt; NDX net debt (deducting reserves) relative to exports of goods and services.
Source: Same as table 10.
a. Eleven largest debtors. For the remaining countries, see appendix table B-2.

dollar depreciation) the decine would be even greater, by 23 percent to $43 billion. The indicators of creditworthiness both show improvement. Thus, the aggregate ratio of net debt (gross debt *minus* reserves) to exports of goods and services falls from 1.87 in 1982 to 1.62 in 1986, and the ratio of debt service (long-term debt amortization and interest on both long- and short-term debt) to exports of goods and services falls from 37 percent in 1982 to 30 percent in 1986. Clearly, the medium-term trend is toward improvement.

There is a sharp difference between oil importers and oil exporters, however. Given the base assumption that the nominal dollar price of oil remains at $29 per barrel in 1983–85 and returns to $34 only by 1986, the current account deficit of the oil exporters grows from $21 billion in 1982

		1982	1983	1984	1985	1986
Philippines	CA	−3,500	−4,110	−3,779	−3,581	−3,946
	D	22,400	26,119	29,614	32,796	36,334
	NDX	2.981	3.080	2.724	2.612	2.607
Indonesia	CA	−6,600	−4,568	−7,318	−9,770	−10,160
	D	21,000	25,844	33,611	43,623	53,948
	NDX	0.895	1.159	1.379	1.725	1.900
Israel	CA	−5,100	−6,815	−7,539	−8,593	−9,890
	D	20,400	27,487	35,433	44,322	54,535
	NDX	1.921	2.398	2.504	2.828	3.187
Turkey	CA	−1,100	−1,375	−577	36	−127
	D	19,000	20,329	20,989	20,935	21,163
	NDX	2.406	2.334	1.921	1.677	1.507
Yugoslavia	CA	−464	−551	830	1,350	1,790
	D	18,477	19,359	19,048	18,077	16,698
	NDX	1.136	1.041	0.797	0.653	0.522
Chile	CA	−2,540	−3,911	−3,479	−3,290	−3,865
	D	18,000	21,730	24,872	27,723	31,159
	NDX	3.003	3.096	2.634	2.551	2.594

to $41 billion in 1986, rising by nearly 60 percent in real terms. The net debt-to-exports ratio for oil exporters rises from 1.77 to 2.36—a high level, comparable to that found today in some of the more indebted Latin American countries; and the debt-service ratio rises from 34 percent to 41 percent.

In contrast, for the oil-importing countries the basic projections show a surprisingly favorable outcome. Their combined current account changes from a deficit $35 billion in 1982 to a deficit of $12.6 billion in 1986. Their net debt-to-exports ratio declines from 1.94 in 1982 to 1.28 in 1986, and their debt-service ratio declines from 39 percent to 26 percent.

Table 11 presents the projections for individual countries in the base case. The projections for Brazil are surprisingly favorable; and for 1983–84 they coincide almost exactly with the government's deficit targets, often considered to be on the optimistic side. Thereafter the deficit continues to decline rapidly.

Although this profile may be somewhat optimistic, it illustrates the progress that could be made with real devaluation and the possible leeway for relatively brisk growth recovery by 1984.[56]

The results for Mexico are favorable for 1983—showing a current account deficit somewhat smaller than the $3.4 billion figure originally called for in the IMF-Mexico program. Nonetheless, the sharp drop in Mexico's imports in the first half of 1983 suggests that the actual outcome may be a deficit smaller than projected here for 1983.

Results for Argentina resemble those for Brazil, suggesting that for two of the three largest debtors the 1984–86 period holds the potential for considerable improvement in external debt pressure. For Korea, the adjusted base case projections indicate a relatively balanced current account even with the assumption of high growth, in part because of a relatively small initial deficit compared to export base. In contrast, even after downward adjustment in growth and substantial depreciation, Venezuela's deficits widen considerably, the consequence of weak oil prices and the virtual absence of nonoil exports.

Among other individual major debtors, Indonesia shows a large deficit emerging, but it begins from a sufficiently strong creditworthiness position that its net debt-to-exports ratio by 1986 is still not implausibly high. The growing debt burden of Israel does raise questions of viability. For its part, Chile shows a relatively large sustained deficit even after country-assumption adjustments, although its exports grow fast enough (because of the sharp response of copper prices to the business cycle) to permit modest improvement in its net debt-to-exports ratio.

Projections in the base case for the other eight countries are shown in appendix table B-2. They show a substantial rise in the deficits and net debt-to-exports ratio of Algeria as well as deterioration for Ecuador; continued deficits and little change in creditworthiness for the Philippines, Egypt, Peru, and Portugal; shift to small deficit or even surplus and improving creditworthiness for Turkey and Thailand; and minimal deficits for Hungary and a surprisingly strong shift to surplus for Romania.

Considering the entire set of individual country projections, discussions with international experts on the specific countries suggest the following

---

56. Brazil's exports rise by 33.7 percent in 1984. This seemingly high increase is composed of the following (multiplicative) elements: constant, −3 percent; OECD growth effect, 9 percent; terms of trade effect, 6.5 percent; inflation, 5 percent; dollar devaluation, 9.5 percent; current devaluation, 0.8 percent; lagged devaluation, 3.75 percent.

TABLE 12 **Sensitivity of projections to industrial-country growth, 1986**
(million dollars and ratios)

Industrial-country growth[a]	Oil importers		Oil exporters		Total	
	Current account	Net debt/ exports	Current account	Net debt/ exports	Current account	Net debt/ exports
A (low)	− 55,730	1.92	− 50,932	2.75	− 106,662	2.20
B	− 39,164	1.64	− 47,008	2.58	− 86,172	1.95
C	− 26,141	1.45	− 43,901	2.47	− 70,042	1.78
D (base case)	− 12,626	1.28	− 40,674	2.36	− 53,300	1.62
E (high)	6,210	1.05	− 36,200	2.20	− 29,990	1.41
Memorandum item						
1982	− 35,451	1.94	− 20,989	1.77	− 56,440	1.87

a. See table 9.

direction of bias, if any. The principal cases of overstated deficits and debt appear to be those of Venezuela, Algeria, and perhaps Israel. For the first two, stagnation of oil prices is the principal cause of large projected deficits. However, in the case of Venezuela the model does not capture the sharp cut in imports already in 1983 resulting from rationing of foreign exchange, and accordingly the projections may understate the scope for import compression. For Algeria there may be increased future exports of natural gas, not reflected in the standard methodology. In the case of Israel, the accumulation of debt is overstated because no allowance is made for official grants, which are likely to average $2 billion or more annually, although the estimated current account deficits are not necessarily overstated.[57]

More modest overstatements of future deficits and debt may occur in the projections for Mexico, Indonesia (where devaluation and budgetary restrictions have taken place and future exports of liquified natural gas are likely), the Philippines, Chile, Peru, Ecuador, and Hungary, on the basis of discussions with country experts. For example, for Hungary, the present IMF program calls for a modest current account surplus for 1983, rather than a deficit

57. Because the large debtor countries recieve little grant assistance as middle-income nations, the model omits such aid. This procedure causes a very modest overstatement of debt accumulation for Mexico, Indonesia, the Philippines, Peru, and Thailand, and negligible overstatement for the other countries. Israel is an extreme exception.

(appendix table B-2), and through the use of import restrictions Hungary seems likely to achieve the targeted surplus.

The only notable cases in which the country projections may understate future current account deficits, on the basis of opinions of various country experts, are those of Thailand and Korea (where finance is available for pursuing faster growth) and Brazil (where recent reliance on Third World markets may mean a greater lag in response of exports to OECD recovery than predicted by the model). Thus, the general thrust of these possible individual-country biases suggests that in the aggregate the deficits projected here may tend to be overstated rather than understated, meaning that general prospects for improvement in debt-servicing capacity may be even more favorable than indicated here.

The influence of OECD growth on the debt problem is examined in table 12, which compares results by ascending growth rates. These results strongly suggest that at least 2½ percent of growth must be achieved in 1984–86 (Case C) in order for the debt problem to improve. At this rate, the aggregate ratio of net debt to exports is only slightly improved by 1984–86, and at lower growth it becomes worse in future years than in 1982. In the case of only 1½ percent growth in the period (Case A), the current account deficit of the 19 countries rises to $107 billion by 1986 and the ratio of net debt to exports from 1.87 in 1982 to 2.20 in 1986. In the event of growth this low, such large potential deficits would be so unlikely to be capable of financing that the diagnosis would have to be one of insolvency rather than illiquidity. Even with the case of 2½ percent growth (Case C) the amounts to be financed are sufficiently large that the question of insolvency versus illiquidity would still be open. With growth of 3 percent, however (base Case D), there is a sufficiently clear trend of declining relative size of deficits and debt that the situation remains manageable, reflecting illiquidity but not insolvency. At higher growth (3½ percent, Case E) the improvement is even sharper.

The strong estimated improvement in developing countries' external accounts in response to higher OECD growth raises the question of whether the projections may be too optimistic because they are based on past relationships that might not apply in the future. Some would argue that terms of trade are unlikely to respond as favorably to OECD growth as in the past, because the inflationary environment of the 1970s has disappeared, and higher real interest rates will work against commodity price recovery. The logic of such concerns is not compelling, however. Higher real interest rates have already reduced commodity inventories, so that the proportionate rise in the amount demanded from this smaller base could be comparable to that found in past experience (or greater if real interest rates subside). Nor is there any reason to believe that the behavior of the general price level (overall inflation) alters the response of relative prices (terms of trade) to OECD growth.

Some analysts contend that because of the greater weight of South-South trade than before, and considering the devastated state of many South-South markets (such as Nigerian demand for Brazilian products), the relationship of developing-country export growth to OECD growth will no longer be as strong as in the past. This concern fails to realize that as country B in the South increases its exports to the OECD it will be able to raise its imports again from country A in the South. Thus, the past relationship should apply, altered at most by a greater time lag.

The projections here do show a sharp rise in export value. In the base case, the dollar value of exports from oil-importing countries is projected to rise by 13 percent in 1983 and 27 percent in 1984, averaging 12 percent growth in 1985–86 (table 10). The surge in 1984 is attributable to dollar depreciation (and resulting increase in the dollar value of trade). But the projections also show relatively rapid increases in dollar values of imports (18 percent in 1984), whereas experience in Mexico and Brazil in 1983 has shown sharp restraint on imports as a form of adjustment.

In short, there is no reason to depart from past relationships of trade volume and terms of trade to OECD growth in projecting external accounts for developing countries in 1983–86. These relationships hold promise for substantial improvement if 3 percent OECD growth is achieved. And to the extent that the estimates of nominal export growth may be biased upward by factors such as assumed dollar depreciation, any such bias is likely to be offset by similar tendencies in the assumed behavior of imports.

The alternative results by OECD growth rate once again show the clear distinction between an improving trend for oil importers and a deteriorating trend for oil exporters. The influence of oil price on developing-country debt is examined in table 13. Under base-case assumptions about other variables, the scenario of low oil price causes the current account deficits of the oil-exporting countries to surge by $19 billion by 1986, raising their net debt-to-exports ratio from 2.36 in the base case for 1986 to a highly risky level of 3.31. Lower prices for oil cause some improvement for oil importers (about $11 billion in 1986 current account), but not as much improvement as the magnitude of deterioration for the oil exporters. Thus, the net debt-to-exports ratio for oil importers by 1986 improves only from 1.28 to 1.14 as the result of the lowering of oil prices between the two scenarios.

The basic reason for these results becomes clearer in table 14, showing

TABLE 13 **Influence of oil price on balance of payments, 19 major debtors, 1982–86**[a]

(million dollars and ratios)

	1982	1983	1984	1985	1986
Expected oil price[b]	34	29	29	29	34
Oil importers					
Oil imports	− 34,499	− 29,426	− 29,426	− 29,426	− 34,499
CA	− 35,451	− 30,890	− 20,207	− 12,564	− 12,626
NDX	1.94	1.88	1.55	1.40	1.28
Oil exporters					
Oil exports	59,140	50,443	40,443	50,443	59,140
CA	− 20,889	− 19,711	− 33,973	− 40,933	− 40,674
NDX	1.77	2.04	2.13	2.35	2.36
Total					
CA	− 56,440	− 50,602	− 54,181	− 53,498	− 53,300
NDX	1.87	1.94	1.74	1.70	1.62
Low oil price[b]	34	20	20	25	25
Oil importers					
Oil imports	− 34,499	− 20,294	− 20,294	− 25,367	− 25,367
CA	− 35,451	− 21,758	− 10,171	− 6,747	− 1,235
NDX	1.94	1.82	1.46	1.29	1.14
Oil exporters					
Oil exports	59,140	34,788	34,788	43,485	43,485
CA	− 20,989	− 35,366	− 51,041	− 50,644	− 59,906
NDX	1.77	2.70	2.93	2.95	3.31
Total					
CA	− 56,440	− 57,124	− 61,213	− 57,391	− 61,141
NDX	1.87	2.10	1.89	1.79	1.77

CA current account; NDX ratio of net debt to exports of goods and services.

a. Base-case assumptions on industrial-country growth, interest rate, and dollar.

b. Dollars per barrel.

the amount of debt and oil trade of the 19 largest debtor countries. As the table shows, oil exports are more vital to the oil exporters (at 78 percent of their exports) than are oil imports to the oil importers (at 31 percent of their imports). To be sure, Turkey, Brazil, and to a lesser extent the Philippines, Israel, and Portugal have a high weight of oil in imports (varying from two-thirds to two-fifths). But overall the proportionate relief to oil importers from a given decline in the price of oil is considerably smaller than the proportionate increased burden of oil exporters.

TABLE 14 **Oil trade by country, 1982**
(million dollars)

	1982 debt	Oil trade	Exports	Oil/exports
Oil importers				
Brazil	88,200	− 10,759	20,175	− .53
Argentina	38,000	0	7,700	0
Korea	35,800	− 5,962	21,761	− .27
Philippines	22,400	− 2,081	4,908	− .42
Israel	20,400	− 2,000	4,741	− .42
Turkey	19,000	− 3,916	5,807	− .67
Yugoslavia	18,477	− 2,511	10,247	− .25
Chile	18,000	− 730	4,044	− .42
Portugal	12,900	− 1,700	3,800	− .19
Thailand	10,500	− 461	6,860	− .07
Romania	8,200	− 3,359	11,715	− .29
Hungary	7,500	− 1,020	8,778	− .12
Total	299,377	− 34,499	110,536	− .31
Oil exporters				
Mexico	82,000	16,477	21,006	.78
Venezuela	31,285	17,315	18,351	.94
Indonesia	21,000	12,238	19,435	.63
Egypt	18,000	3,000	3,404	.88
Algeria	15,093	8,477	8,504	1.00
Peru	11,100	449	3,200	.14
Ecuador	6,300	1,184	2,400	.49
Total	184,778	59,140	76,300	.78
Total, 19 countries	484,155	24,641	186,836	n.a.

n.a. Not applicable.
Source: Tables 11, B-2; *International Financial Statistics,* and national sources.

This analysis suggests that a major area for possible debt risk to the system is the growing debt of oil exporters, especially if oil prices collapse. The analysis here contradicts the view often expressed, including by some official sources, that sharply lower oil prices would tend to be good for developing countries and their debt problems because they are largely oil importers. That view reflects lack of recognition that the major debtors as a group are oil exporters on balance (table 14), and that the effects of oil price changes are much more concentrated for oil exporters than for oil importers. Part of the difficulty with the conventional perception is the tendency to conduct analysis for "nonoil developing countries" while treating OPEC countries separately. Yet the standard classification of "nonoil developing country" includes Mexico, Egypt, and Peru (as well as some other oil exporters); and the OPEC grouping includes countries that are appropriately defined as developing and not in capital surplus: Algeria, Ecuador, Nigeria (omitted here), Indonesia, and Venezuela.

Although a detailed analysis of the impact of lower oil prices is beyond the scope of this study, the question is of sufficient policy importance to warrant carrying the analysis a step further to incorporate indirect effects. A controversial issue preceding the OPEC price reduction in March 1983 was whether a collapse in the price of oil would improve or seriously worsen the problem of international debt.[58] The estimates in table 13 indicate that, in terms of direct impact, sharply lower oil prices would tend to aggravate the debt problem, on balance. However, there would be mitigating indirect effects. Lower oil prices would tend to stimulate economic growth in industrial countries and reduce inflation and therefore nominal interest rates. The OECD has estimated that a decline of 10 percent in the price of oil (or $3.30 per barrel, in 1982 when the estimate was prepared) causes an increase in OECD growth by 0.2 percent in each of the two succeeding years.[59] The Congressional Budget Office has calculated that a decline by $8 per barrel in the price of oil would reduce US inflation by an average of 0.75 percentage points, and reduce interest rates by an average of 0.68 percentage points, over four years.[60]

The scenario for low oil prices examined in table 13 considers an average

58. See, for example, *Wall Street Journal*, 24 and 26 January 1983.

59. OECD *Economic Outlook* (31 July 1982), p. 139.

60. US Congress, Congressional Budget Office, "Economic and Budgetary Consequences of an Oil Price Decline—A Preliminary Analysis" (Washington, March 1983; processed), p. 15.

reduction of approximately $8 per barrel in 1983–86 from the path in the base case. Applying this reduction to the relationships just cited, the consequence of lower oil prices would be an increase in the OECD growth rate (by 0.48 percent) in 1983 and 1984, lower interest rates, and lower inflation. If the base-case assumptions are adjusted accordingly, it is possible to examine the total impact of lower oil prices after taking account of induced stimulus to OPEC growth and moderation of interest rates and inflation.[61] Incorporation of these feedback effects under lower oil prices causes the 1986 current account deficit of oil-exporting countries to decline by 9.3 percent relative to the estimates with direct effects only (from $59.9 billion, table 13, to $54.3 billion) and pushes the oil-importing countries into current account surplus (from − $1.2 billion to + $6.6 billion). After incorporating these beneficial feedback effects, a drop in the price of oil reduces the current account deficit of the 19 countries as a whole in comparison to the base case (from $53.5 billion at expected oil prices to $47.7 billion at lower oil prices after inclusion of feedback effects).

In sum, once indirect effects in OECD growth and interest rates are incorporated, a sharp drop in the price of oil would tend to reduce the current account deficit of the developing countries considered as a group. Nonetheless, such a drop would still tend to aggravate the severity of the debt problem because its adverse effects on oil-exporting countries would be relatively greater than its beneficial effects on oil-importing countries. Thus, in the base case (higher oil prices) by 1986 the ratio of net debt to exports is 1.28 for oil importers and 2.36 for oil exporters (table 10). A decline in the oil price alone changes these ratios to 1.14 and 3.31, more seriously aggravating the debt burden of oil exporters than alleviating it for oil importers. Incorporation of beneficial indirect effects from induced OECD growth and lower interest rates only improves these 1986 ratios to 1.03 and 3.15, respectively. Considering that these ratios still show an extremely high burden for oil exporters and only moderate further improvement for oil importers, the conclusion of adverse impact of sharply lower oil prices on the debt burden remains essentially unchanged.

The debt problem is also sensitive to the level of international interest rates. Much of existing debt is at variable interest rates linked to LIBOR.

---

61. The adjusted scenario applies base-case assumptions except as follows (1983–86, respectively): OECD growth, 1.98 percent, 3.48 percent, 3.0 percent, 3.0 percent; LIBOR: 9.1 percent, 8.3 percent, 7.4 percent, 7.5 percent; inflation: 3.7 percent, 4.2 percent, 4.3 percent, 4.8 percent; oil price: $20, $20, $25, $25.

As shown in table 15, under a scenario of high interest rates (averaging 13.5 percent in 1983–86 instead of 8.75 percent as in the base case), the total current account deficit of the 19 largest debtors is approximately $29 billion larger by 1986, and the ratio of net debt to exports shows much less improvement (from 1.87 to 1.81) than in the base case (1.87 to 1.62). As the table indicates, with the 1982 debt base a 1 percent interest increase (1983) causes $2.73 billion increase in net interest payments by this group of countries.[62]

TABLE 15   **Influence of interest rates on balance of payments, 19 major debtor countries, 1982–86**[a]
(percentage and million dollars)

	1982	1983	1984	1985	1986
Expected LIBOR					
(percentage)	15	10	9	8	8
Interest	− 44,887	− 45,775	− 46,944	− 47,896	− 51,471
CA	− 56,440	− 50,602	− 54,181	− 53,498	− 53,300
NDX	1.87	1.94	1.74	1.70	1.62
D	484,155	529,153	581,340	628,585	675,654
High LIBOR					
(percentage)	15	11	13	15	15
Interest	− 44,887	− 48,509	− 59,087	− 72,064	− 80,412
CA	− 56,440	− 53,336	− 66,324	− 77,666	− 82,241
NDX	1.87	1.95	1.79	1.81	1.81
D	484,155	531,887	596,218	667,631	743,641

CA current account; NDX ratio of net debt to exports of goods and services; D total debt.
a. Under base-case assumptions on industrial-country growth, oil price, and the dollar.

Comparing tables 12 and 15, an interest rate 4.75 percentage points higher on average over 1983–86 causes a $29 billion deterioration in current account by 1986, while a 0.75 percentage point decline in OECD growth causes approximately $33 billion deterioration (Case B compared with Case D in

62. For all 19 countries debt is $484.6 billion and reserves are $46.4 billion. Allowing for higher earnings on reserves, the response of interest payments to a 1 percent change in interest, shown in table 15, implies that 62 percent of total debt is indexed to LIBOR.

table 12). Thus, on average one percentage point change in OECD growth is seven times as powerful as each percentage point change in the interest rate in remedying the debt problem.[63] This relationship varies by country types. For countries with especially large debt relative to exports, interest rates have somewhat more effect. Thus, for Brazil and Argentina one percentage point on OECD growth has the equivalent impact of 5.7 and 4.5 percentage points in the interest rate, respectively, somewhat smaller than the average relationship. For oil exporters, whose principal export does not respond to OECD growth (in the model as formulated), the relative growth impact is even smaller; one percentage point in OECD growth is the equivalent of 2.7 percentage points on interest for Mexico and 3.2 percentage points on interest for all oil exporters. Despite these differences, a percentage point increase in growth is much more favorable than a percentage point cut in the interest rate for all of the countries examined (the ratio reaches 10 to 1 for oil importers as a group).

This pattern has major implications for macroeconomic policy in OECD countries. It means that it would be better for the problem of developing-country debt to achieve higher average, sustained growth in industrial countries even at some modest cost in increased interest rates. Moderate expansion would be preferable to hypercautious slower growth even at the price of some rise in interest rates. At the same time, the larger relative impact of one percentage point of growth than of the interest rate also tends to mitigate concern about the mid-1983 upward creep in US interest rates in pursuit of more moderate but sustainable monetary growth (following several months of rapid monetary growth), for the purpose of ensuring more sustainable (and therefore higher average) real growth.

Holding growth rates constant, however, the central thrust of the interest-rate analysis is that higher interest rates would greatly burden the debt situation, pushing it further from illiquidity toward insolvency. A crucial implication of this assessment is that in the choice of macroeconomic tools to achieve recovery, the industrial countries would do far better to choose policy mixes that tend to have lower rather than higher interest rates (looser

---

63. Based on the model's equations, 1 percent OECD growth raises exports of goods and services by 3 percent in volume, and by an average of approximately 3 percent in price, for a total of 6 percent export increase. Considering that net debt is 1.87 times exports of goods and services, and that two-thirds of the debt is indexed to LIBOR, a 1 percent reduction in interest rate cuts interest payments by 1.2 percent of exports of goods and services. On the basis of these parameters, without adjustment for differing weights of countries, a 1 percent rise in OECD growth would have an impact equivalent to a 5 percentage point reduction in LIBOR.

monetary policy and tighter fiscal policy rather than the reverse), for a given result in terms of real growth.

The final dimension of the model's sensitivity concerns the strength of the dollar. There is widespread sentiment that the dollar has been unduly strong compared with long-run equilibrium, primarily as the result of high US interest rates, "safe-haven" capital inflows, and other factors.[64] In 1983 the US current account deficit is expected to increase sharply, and by past experience the consequence will eventually be a decline in the value of the dollar—although higher interest rates caused by fiscal deficits could forestall that decline.

TABLE 16 **Influence of dollar strength on balance of payments and debt, 19 major debtor countries, 1982–86**[a]

(million dollars)

	1982	1983	1984	1985	1986
Expected dollar					
index[b]	1.00	1.05	1.15	1.15	1.15
CA	− 56,440	− 50,602	− 54,181	− 53,498	− 53,300
NDX	1.87	1.94	1.74	1.70	1.62
D	484,155	529,153	581,340	628,585	675,654
Strong dollar					
index[b]	1.00	1.00	1.05	1.05	1.05
CA	− 56,440	− 49,371	− 51,123	− 50,208	− 49,795
NDX	1.87	2.01	1.87	1.81	1.73
D	484,155	527,190	575,091	619,575	663,763

CA current account; NDX ratio of net debt to exports of goods and services; D total debt.

a. Under base-case assumptions about industrial-country growth, oil price, and interest rates.

b. Higher index indicates real depreciation.

Table 16 reports the response of the base-case estimates to a smaller rather than larger dollar depreciation. In the base case the dollar depreciates relative to other major currencies by 5 percent in 1983 and another 10 percent in

64. For example, see John Williamson, *The Exchange Rate System*, POLICY ANALYSES IN INTERNATIONAL ECONOMICS 5 (Washington: Institute for International Economics, forthcoming 1983).

1984; in the alternative case it does not depreciate until 1984, and then only by 5 percent. A stronger dollar actually causes lower current account deficits in dollar terms and lower dollar debt; but because it reduces the dollar value of exports, it causes a less favorable creditworthiness position as measured by net debt relative to exports. Thus, by 1986, the aggregate ratio of net debt to exports of goods and services declines from 1.87 to 1.62 in the base case, but only to 1.73 in the strong-dollar scenario. Thus, greater precariousness of developing-country debt is another concern that may be added to that of severe US trade imbalances (and resulting macroeconomic sluggishness as well as protectionist pressure) caused by an overly strong dollar. This evaluation reinforces the earlier conclusion that interest rates, as least US interest rates, should be brought down (through reduced fiscal deficits) to facilitate the management of debt, because high US interest rates have contributed importantly to a strong dollar.

Finally, among the 40 possible combinations in the model estimates (5 growth scenarios, 2 oil cases, 2 LIBOR, and 2 dollar cases), it is perhaps worth reporting the best-case and worst-case results. In the best case examined, growth averages 3.1 percent in 1983–86, LIBOR averages 8¾ percent, the oil price holds at $29 per barrel, and the dollar depreciates by 15 percent. Under these assumptions, the aggregate current account deficit falls to $30 billion by 1986, and the net debt-to-exports ratio falls from 1.87 in 1982 to 1.41. In the worst case (average growth of 1.4 percent, average LIBOR of 13.5 percent, oil price falling to $20 in 1983–84, and dollar depreciation of only 5 percent), by 1986 the aggregate current account deficit reaches $138 billion ($75 billion for oil exporters alone) and the net debt-to-exports ratio rises from 1.87 to 2.78 (and reaches 4.11 for oil exporters). Under the worst case the debt clearly cannot be managed and bankruptcy proceedings to deal with insolvency are in order. Clearly, the international debt problem contains major downside risk even though the central analysis here suggests that in the expected, base case it is manageable.

As a summary evaluation of the central projections of this study, it is useful to compare the portion of debt held by those countries whose situations improve by 1986 to that held by those whose situations deteriorate. Judging performance by the trend in the ratio of net debt to exports, this compilation yields the following results. Under base-case conditions (3 percent growth in 1984–86), the following countries register an improvement in their debt situation: Brazil, Mexico, Argentina, Korea, the Philippines, Turkey, Yugoslavia, Chile, Portugal, Thailand, Romania, and Hungary, with total 1982 debt of $361 billion. The remaining countries show deterioration by 1986:

Venezuela, Indonesia, Israel, Egypt, Algeria, Peru, and Ecuador, with a total of $123 billion in 1982 debt. Thus, for 75 percent of outstanding debt the base case indicates improvement over the next four years.

Reviewing those countries that show deterioration, the net debt-to-exports ratios reach the following levels by 1986: Venezuela, 2.6; Indonesia, 1.9; Israel, 3.2; Egypt, 2.4 (almost unchanged from 1982); Algeria, 2.7; Peru, 2.7; and Ecuador, 2.6. Of these countries, Indonesia is the only one with a sufficiently low projected ratio of net debt to exports to suggest scope for avoiding debt difficulties. The others all show projected ratios which, though well below the levels of Brazil and Argentina in their 1982 crises, are not substantially different from the levels of other countries that did experience debt-rescheduling difficulties in 1982 (notably Mexico, 2.7 in 1982, and Ecuador, 2.0).

Other recent studies have reached the same general conclusions as those found here. Recent studies by Morgan Guaranty bank reach similar conclusions, despite some difference in individual country estimates.[65] The International Monetary Fund has projected that for the nonoil developing countries current account deficits will decline from 19.3 percent of export earnings in 1982 to 14 percent by 1986.[66] While pointing in the same direction as those of the present study, the IMF projections show less improvement than estimated here. Thus, the 19 countries examined here would experience a decline in the ratio of their current account deficit to exports of goods and services from 24.2 percent in 1982 to 14.3 percent in 1986, a sharper reduction than that foreseen by the IMF. On the other hand, the Morgan Guaranty forecasts imply an even stronger reduction in deficits than estimated here (table 20, page 109).

A more precise evaluation of the degree of improvement in the burden of developing-country debt is possible through the application of a statistical model of debt rescheduling.[67] Using logit statistical analysis, I have estimated

---

65. *World Financial Markets* (February 1983), pp. 1–11, and (June 1983), pp. 1–15. For 21 major debtor countries, Morgan Guaranty estimates that in 1985 the ratio of debt to exports will be 166 percent; the estimate here for 19 major debtors in 1986 is 162 percent for the ratio of net debt to exports. However, Morgan Guaranty has considerably more pessimistic estimates for Argentina and Brazil (302 percent and 333 percent, respectively, versus 180 percent and 197 percent in this study) and a more optimistic estimate for Chile (187 percent versus 259 percent).

66. IMF *World Economic Outlook*, 1983, p. 205.

67. William R. Cline, "A Logit Model of Debt Rescheduling, 1967–82," *International Debt.*

TABLE 17 **Projections of logit indicator of debt-servicing difficulties,[a] 19 major debtor countries, 1980–86**

	1980	1981	1982	1983	1984	1985	1986
Brazil	0.026	0.747	0.810	0.999	0.909	0.402	0.144
Mexico	0.135	0.021	0.435	0.949	0.679	0.241	0.129
Argentina	0.000	0.002	0.311	0.691	0.730	0.121	0.026
Korea	0.027	0.004	0.027	0.004	0.002	0.001	0.001
Venezuela	0.000	0.000	0.000	0.000	0.000	0.000	0.001
Philippines	0.002	0.001	0.050	0.265	0.406	0.133	0.073
Indonesia	0.000	0.000	0.001	0.015	0.010	0.008	0.011
Israel	0.003	0.004	0.033	0.018	0.056	0.042	0.063
Turkey	n.a.	n.a.	0.542	0.189	0.189	0.066	0.031
Yugoslavia	0.009	0.007	n.a.	0.074	0.041	0.011	0.005
Chile	0.000	0.000	0.265	0.650	0.369	0.105	0.051
Egypt	0.049	0.009	0.197	0.604	0.467	0.202	0.148
Algeria	0.003	0.001	n.a.	0.178	0.050	0.109	0.322
Portugal	0.002	0.016	0.164	0.447	0.263	0.073	0.036
Peru	n.a.	0.000	n.a.	0.095	0.220	0.094	0.074
Thailand	0.001	0.001	0.024	0.021	0.011	0.003	0.002
Romania	0.018	0.020	0.054	0.015	0.006	0.002	0.001
Hungary	n.a.	n.a.	n.a.	0.012	0.005	0.002	0.001
Ecuador	0.000	0.000	0.051	0.788	0.669	0.459	0.483

a. Critical level: 0.242.

a model explaining the occurrence of debt reschedulings in the period 1967–82 for approximately 60 countries. The model shows that debt rescheduling is associated with a high debt-service ratio, low ratio of reserves to imports, low rate of amortization, high current account deficit, low domestic growth rates, and a low level of international lending in relative terms. A composite indicator of debt-servicing difficulty using this model yields the projected values shown in table 17, with a critical index level of 0.242, such that projected levels in excess of this threshold mean the country's debt-servicing difficulties are likely to be severe and comparable to those of past debt reschedulings.

As shown in table 17, the debt-servicing burden is likely to remain above the critical index level associated with reschedulings in Brazil through 1985, Mexico and Argentina through 1984, Chile through 1984, and Ecuador through 1986. Otherwise the projections show few instances of serious debt-servicing difficulties, especially by 1985–86.

While the projections of the composite indicator of debt-servicing difficulty tend to confirm the analysis here of prospective improvement, they do signal the need for special arrangements for certain major debtor countries over the interim period when borrowing on a fully normal basis of voluntary lending is likely to be infeasible. For this reason, the process of "involuntary lending" analyzed in section 4 is of special importance. Banks that already have substantial exposure in Argentina, Brazil, and Mexico are likely to continue providing new lending to them on a quasi-involuntary basis to secure the safety of the previous loans, until there is sufficient improvement that lending can return to a fully voluntary basis.

As a final check on the feasibility of the projections of this study, it is important to consider their implications for domestic savings and consumption potential. A central feature of the base-case projection is that the current account deficit of oil-importing countries declines substantially (from $35.5 billion in 1982 to $12.6 billion in 1986, table 10). Yet their interest payments remain high (at approximately $30 billion). Accordingly, the net foreign resource transfer to them declines, implying lower availability of external savings to finance growth. The question arises as to whether this scenario is feasible, given the implication that either domestic growth would have to decline or that domestic savings rates would have to rise as the consequence of lower savings provided from abroad. The feasibility of this projection depends in part on the political sustainability of adjustment programs, and that sustainability depends on the severity of cuts in consumption that might be required by a decline in the resource transfer.

The net resource transfer to a country *equals* its net capital inflow (including direct investment) *plus* its transfers received *minus* its net interest and profits paid abroad. By balance of payments identities, this net resource transfer also *equals* the current account deficit *minus* interests payments abroad *plus* transfers *plus* increases in reserves.[68] From appendix table B-3, for 12 oil-importing countries this calculation shows net resource transfers falling from $11.2 billion in 1982 to $7.0 billion in 1986. Note that the decline in net resource transfer is smaller than would be suspected by examining the

---

68. If RT = resource transfer, K = capital account, I = net interest payments receipts less payments, and Tr = private transfers, then $RT = K + I + Tr$. By balance of payments definition, $K = -CA + \Delta R$ where K is capital account balance, CA is current account balance, and ΔR is change in reserve. Therefore $RT = (-CA + \Delta R) + I + Tr = -CA + I + Tr + \Delta R$, as the text states.

declining current account deficit alone; the primary reason is that in 1982 there was a substantial loss of reserves while in 1986 reserves are projected to rise. In other words, a significant portion of the current account deficit in 1982 was financed by reserve loss rather than capital outflow.

In relation to gross national product, the net resource transfer to the 12 oil-importing countries is projected to decline from 1.41 percent of their GNP in 1982 to 0.53 percent in 1986.[69] Assuming standard relations between incremental savings and GNP, a decline of this magnitude (0.88 percent of GNP) would decrease GNP growth by 0.3 percent of GNP annually, unless offset by increased domestic savings. However, these magnitudes are sufficiently modest that adjustment to them should be feasible; as part of concerted efforts to adjust to foreign sector difficulties, it should be possible for countries to raise their domestic savings rates by 0.88 percent of GNP or to accept reduced growth by 0.3 percent annually. Accordingly, the projections of table 10 should not prove infeasible from the standpoint of imposing an insurmountable burden of reduced resource transfer. As for the oil-exporting countries, the net resource transfer rises substantially in the base case (from −$9.8 billion in 1982 to +$24.6 billion in 1986), so that the question of feasibility of domestic acceptance of reduction in resource transfer does not arise.

Implications

The estimates of this section indicate that a critical threshold for industrial-country growth in 1984–86 is 3 percent annually. If this growth rate can be achieved, the debt problems of the developing countries should be manageable and should show considerable improvement. The estimates encompass 19 countries accounting for two-thirds of total debt of developing and East European countries. The central result of this analysis is that the debt problem can be managed, and that it is essentially a problem of illiquidity, not insolvency. Thus, the final estimates show the aggregate current account deficit declining from 1982 to 1986 by 23 percent in real terms. The ratio of the current account deficit to exports of goods and services declines from 24 percent in 1982 to 14 percent in 1986, and the ratio of net debt to exports

---

69. GNP for 1982 is based on World Bank, *World Development Report 1983*, pp. 148–49, as adjusted for 1981–82 growth and inflation; for 1986 it is based on the growth, inflation, and dollar devaluation assumptions of the model presented in this section.

of goods and services declines from 1.87 to 1.62. Countries accounting for three-fourths of the total debt of the 19 countries examined show improving trends toward reduced relative debt burdens.

There could nonetheless be protracted problems in individual countries. Oil exporters tend to experience deteriorating debt trends. On a basis of trends in current account and ratio of debt to exports, countries such as Venezuela, Algeria, Israel, and Egypt, could enter into new or more severe debt problems, while Ecuador and Peru could face continuation or intensi- fication of existing debt-rescheduling problems (subject to the qualifications on possible direction of bias in individual country estimates, as noted above).

The analysis of this section is based on the outlook for countries with large external debt. Many smaller countries have experienced debt-servicing difficulties. In the aggregate, nonetheless, the debts of smaller countries with debt-servicing disruptions are small relative to global debt totals. Except for special problems that might arise in individual banks with unusually high exposure in an individual small country, there is little potential systemic threat from even the aggregate debt of the smaller debt countries with debt difficulties.

From another standpoint, however, they could affect the system. Some countries not analyzed in the projections here have gone beyond normal multilateral debt reschedulings and have deferred interest payments, including Poland, Nicaragua, and Costa Rica. It is possible that their actions gradually could build a precedent that could spread to large-debt countries, with systemic consequences. This possibility should remain unlikely, however, as long as the expected improving trends in large-country debt actually mater- ialize. The major debtor countries consistently have shown their desire to demonstrate their superior creditworthiness and unwillingness to be grouped indiscriminately with other developing countries in creditworthiness evalua- tion, and unless seriously pressed by deteriorating external positions or domestic political unrest, the major debtor countries would be unlikely to imitate the more drastic, nonmarket rescheduling actions and demands of some of the smaller countries.

Some of the implications of this study for industrial-country policy are self-evident: the achievement of faster growth and lower interest rates is crucial to resolving debt problems. Other implications are less obvious: a less overvalued dollar would help alleviate the debt problem; and a collapse in oil prices would seriously worsen the debt problem.

The appropriate policy measures to achieve the critical threshold of 3 percent OECD growth should include reduction in out-year budget deficits to permit adequately expansionary monetary policy in the United States, and more expansionary macroeconomic policies of varying mixes in other industrial countries.[70] It is by no means assured that without a shift in macroeconomic policies a growth rate of 3 percent will be achieved. Indeed, simulations with the University of Pennsylvania LINK model show that policy changes of the type just described would raise OECD growth by one-half of a percentage point annually through 1986, boosting growth successfully above a 3 percent threshold that otherwise might not be met.[71]

The most difficult policy question is whether on balance the results indicate that the system can continue with business as usual, aided by case-by-case rescue packages where needed, or whether the risk of generalized "insolvency" is so great that more sweeping reform is required. The answer to this question must be that, because the chances are good for adequate global recovery, the debt will indeed be manageable, and therefore that it would be counterproductive to adopt, out of unnecessary panic, sweeping debt reform measures that might have adverse effects of their own; but that the underlying risk of insolvency is sufficient that it cannot be ignored and that at least contingency planning should be in progress so that policymakers would be prepared to deal with the less favorable outcomes if they materialized.

4   Debt Dynamics: Involuntary Lending, Rescheduling, and Default Incentives

The preceding analysis suggests that in the medium term under reasonable world economic recovery, the problem of international debt can be managed without serious systemic breakdown. However, the analysis also indicates that for at least some key debtor countries there will be an interim period

---

70. *Promoting World Recovery: A Statement on Global Economic Strategy* by Twenty-six Economists from Fourteen Countries (Washington: Institute for International Economics, December 1982).

71. C. Fred Bergsten and Lawrence R. Klein, "Assuring World Recovery: The Need for a Global Strategy," *The Economist*, 23 April 1983.

during which access to capital markets on a voluntary basis will be highly unlikely, requiring instead continued financing on a quasi-involuntary basis by banks that already have a stake in the country. The dynamics of "involuntary lending" are examined in this section to determine whether this process is likely to be viable.

Because reschedulings are currently a major instrument for dealing with debt problems and may remain so during an interim period, the discussion also considers the lessons that have been learned about rescheduling techniques. The discussion closes with an examination of the incentives and disincentives to country default, considering that an option open to borrowers is to declare their unwillingness to continue servicing their debt.

Involuntary Lending

An important element in sovereign lending since August 1982 has been the phenomenon of forced lending. Forced, or involuntary, lending may be defined as the increase in a bank's exposure to a borrowing nation that is in debt-servicing difficulty and that, because of a loss of creditworthiness, would be unable to attract new lending from banks not already exposed in the country. Perhaps the purest example is the case of Mexico. After suspension of its debt-servicing payments in August 1982, Mexico was able to secure an across-the-board 7 percent increase in the exposure of foreign banks as part of a financial package for 1983. The leadership of the International Monetary Fund, indeed, its ultimatum to the banks that in the absence of their increased exposure IMF funds would not be forthcoming, played an instrumental role in this process. Similar operations of IMF-led bank lending under less than voluntary circumstances have been carried out in Argentina and Brazil, and, to some extent, in Chile, Peru, and Yugoslavia. The total amount of new lending extended in this mode within the last year is on the order of $15 billion—meaning that for 1983 perhaps half or more of total new net bank lending to developing countries will be of the involuntary variety.

Basically, banks are willing to extend new loans in such circumstances because they are in a "lender's trap": they must extend new money in order to shore up the quality of their previous, outstanding loans. Ironically, under current conditions of the international financial market, the lender's trap plays a role that is highly productive in social terms: it helps ensure a source of new lending to countries that are broadly cut off from other sources of private credit because of perceived risk and debt-servicing difficulties.

The basic dynamic of forced lending is that the lender with existing exposure will increase the exposure with new loans as long as the new funds are judged likely to enable a firming-up of the previous exposure rather than to be merely a throwing of good money after bad. Existing lenders will provide new lending if the benefits exceed the costs. The cost of new lending in a risky situation is the risk that it will be lost in default. The benefit of new lending is the value received from shoring up the old loans.

Lenders will provide additional new loans as long as (a) the reduction in the probability of country default thereby achieved, *multiplied by* previously outstanding loans, *exceeds* (b) the terminal probability of default (after the new loans) as *multiplied by* the amount of the new loans. The amount (a) is the expected (probability-weighted) benefit of new lending, while the amount (b) is its expected cost.[72]

The net benefit of new, forced lending, relative to the amount of existing debt, depends therefore on the degree of initial default risk, terminal default risk, and ratio of new loans to previous exposure. Ironically, the incentive for forced lending is greater for a higher initial probability of default, *given* a specific terminal level of default, because the resulting reduction in default risk is greater. The incentive for forced lending is higher for a *lower* terminal probability of default. And it is higher if the relative increase in exposure required (new lending relative to previous exposure) is smaller.

The case of Mexico perhaps illustrates the process. The probability of default in the absence of new lending was substantial; the probability of default that could be achieved if the new funds could be mobilized was low; and the requirement of new lending relative to exposure was moderate (7 percent).

To examine the strength of the incentive for forced lending under alternative

---

72. Thus, if the amount of outstanding exposure is D, the initial probability of default is P_0, the amount of the new lending is L, and the probability of default thereafter is P_1 the lender will extend the new loans as long as:

(1) $(P_0 - P_1)D > P_1L$.

That is, new lending will be extended if the reduction in probability of default thereby achieved $(P_0 - P_1)$, *times* outstanding debt (D), *exceeds* the new (lower) probability of default (P_1), *times* the extra capital placed at risk (new lending, L). Expressed as a fraction of outstanding debt, the net benefit from new lending is therefore:

(2) $B = [(P_0 - P_1)D - P_1L]/D = P_0 - P_1[1 + (L/D)]$.

TABLE 18 **Expected net benefit from additional lending under duress**
(net benefit as a fraction of outstanding exposure)

Case	New lending/ debt	Original default probability	Decline in default probability			
			.1	.2	.3	
A	.07	.2	.093	.200	n.a.	n.a.
		.4	.079	.186	.293	.400
		.5	.072	.179	.286	.393
		.6	.065	.172	.279	.386
		.8	.051	.158	.265	.372
B	.15	.2	.085	.200	n.a.	n.a.
		.4	.055	.170	.285	.400
		.5	.040	.155	.270	.385
		.6	.025	.140	.255	.370
		.8	−.005	.110	.225	.340
C	.20	.2	.080	.200	n.a.	n.a.
		.4	.040	.160	.280	.400
		.5	.020	.140	.260	.380
		.6	.000	.120	.240	.360
		.8	−.040	.080	.200	.320
D	.30	.2	.070	.200	n.a.	n.a.
		.4	.010	.140	.270	.400
		.5	−.020	.110	.240	.370
		.6	−.050	.080	.210	.340
		.8	−.110	.020	.150	.280
E	.40	.2	.060	.200	n.a.	n.a.
		.4	−.020	.120	.260	.400
		.5	−.060	.080	.220	.360
		.6	−.100	.040	.180	.320
		.8	−.180	−.040	.100	.240

n.a. Not applicable: default probability cannot be below zero.

conditions, table 18 sets forth numerical examples of the net benefits as a fraction of outstanding exposure (equation 2 of note 72), under alternative assumptions about initial default probability, change in default probability achieved, and relative magnitude of new lending compared with previous exposure.

The strong pattern shown in table 18 is that under rather extreme conditions it may still be beneficial to extend new loans. Considering first more modest new lending, if banks expand exposure by 7 percent (Case A) their expected (probability-weighted) benefit will be between 5 percent and 9 percent of existing exposure if a decline in default probability of only 10 percent is achieved, rising to nearly a 40 percent benefit if a 40 percent reduction in default probability is achieved. Moving to larger new lending, if the improvement in default probability is limited to 10 percent, the conditions for extending new lending become more stringent (lending will occur only at lower original default probabilities) as the size of new lending relative to exposure rises. Thus, banks will not find it beneficial on balance to lend 30 percent beyond existing exposure if the initial default probability is 50 percent and the decline in default productivity thereby achieved is only 10 percent. However, for larger declines in default probability, even large amounts of new lending relative to exposure are beneficial. Thus, there is only one case of net loss at 20 percent reduction in default probability, and for higher achievable reductions, the whole range of new lending and original default risk yields positive expected results from additional lending.

In some of the crucial debtor cases, the absence of new bank lending is likely to trigger extended moratorium, if not once-for-all default. The simple analysis proposed here does not capture moratorium as opposed to default. But an extended moratorium may be conceived of as a partial default— perhaps a 20 percent to 40 percent expected default. The extension of new lending may be thought of as largely eliminating the risk of extended moratorium. Accordingly, it might be proper to think of this reduction of default-equivalent as perhaps 10 to 20 percentage points, the first two columns of the table. As for the amounts of new lending, none of the major rescue operations has involved expansion of bank exposure by as much as 20 percent, and indeed this percentage might be the total expected over a full two- to three-year horizon of involuntary lending. Thus, in practice, the relevant portion of the table is probably the first two columns and first three rows. It is striking that in this set of 30 possibilities, in only two cases will the new lending have an expected cost in excess of expected benefits (cases B and C with original probability of default = 0.8 and change in default probability = 0.1).

In sum, a simple model of involuntary lending suggests that over the range of most relevant situations likely to arise—except in cases of relatively clear country insolvency—it will pay the banks to extend additional credit in order to secure the value of existing exposure. The process of involuntary lending should be relatively reliable as a source of continued capital flow during the interim period before the country can return to capital markets on a basis of normal creditworthiness and fully voluntary bank lending.

Free Riders

The above analysis treats all banks that are exposed in a country as a single decision unit. In practice, however, many banks are involved, and especially the smaller ones among them have an incentive to take advantage of the increased quality of their outstanding loans obtained through new lending by the larger banks without incurring additional risk by extending new loans themselves.

This "free-rider problem" is a well-known phenomenon in group action. Principal actors in a group that take action in their own behalf confer an external benefit on other actors that do not themselves carry out similar action. These marginal actors are "free riders" in the sense that they participate in a common benefit without bearing any of its cost. The standard solution to this problem is to find ways of marshalling cooperative action by all beneficiaries. Concentration is helpful: for example, it is easier for a highly concentrated industry dominated by a few large producers to mobilize funds for lobbying efforts than for an industry with many small producers and low concentration.

In the case of bank lending to developing countries, some concentration exists (the 9 largest banks account for 60 percent of US bank loans to developing countries), but there is a sufficient weight of numerous, medium-sized banks in total lending flows that the free-rider problem is not easily resolved by concentration alone. Thus, in the case of Brazil it requires 125 international banks to reach coverage of 90 percent of outstanding loans.

The new role of the International Monetary Fund has been crucial for this reason. In the cases of Argentina, Brazil, and Mexico, the IMF insisted that banks provide additional lending as part of the rescue packages. In a sense, the IMF acted as a unifying vehicle to internalize for the banks as a whole the external benefits that the rescue package would confer on them. It acted as a highly effective coordinator capable of marshalling joint action that the large banks by themselves would have had much more difficulty in securing.

In terms of the model of involuntary lending set forth above, the essential problem is that the small bank perceives that its individual action will have no influence on the probability of default, meaning the condition for new lending is not met. Only a smaller group of large banks will recognize that their individual action (broadly coordinated) will affect default probability. But even for them, there will be a smaller improvement in default probability than would exist under a situation of a monopoly bank or completely coordinated set of banks, because the failure of the smaller banks to cooperate will mean that the new amount lent will be smaller.

The central problem then is to ensure uniform collective action, including by regional and smaller banks. Neither is this goal somehow unfair to the smaller banks. On the contrary, if it is not achieved, the nonparticipating smaller banks benefit at the expense of the larger banks (and the IMF) because they enjoy the benefit of increased quality of their outstanding exposure without bearing their fair share of the burden of increased exposure.

By mid-1983 the experience of involuntary lending had shown mixed results on the feasibility of obtaining coordinated action to overcome the free-rider problem. For Mexico, virtually all 530 foreign banks with exposure had increased their exposure by 7 percent.[73] But for Brazil, even the 125 participating banks had failed fully to fulfill the package—especially in the commitment to maintain interbank deposits in foreign branches of Brazilian banks. In this part of the package erosion has been evident in the US regional banks and some European banks.

Moreover, it is unclear how willing the smaller banks will be to repeat involuntary lending in the future. Smaller banks that went along with increased exposure for one year may become increasingly reluctant to do so if involuntary lending has to persist for a second, third, or even fourth year.

There are three basic ways to enforce joint action and overcome the free-rider problem. The first is through official pressure. The IMF has played an important role. In addition, however, there is the possibility of pressure from central banks. This channel appears to have been exercised the most in the United Kingdom, where there is a strong tradition of moral suasion by the Bank of England in times of crisis. In the United States, perceptions appear to differ sharply on the extent of pressure by the Federal Reserve—with at least some of the regional banks having the impression that the Fed could be uncooperative in future individual bank difficulties if these banks do not cooperate on the debt problem.[74] Nonetheless, there are limits to the use of

---

73. *Wall Street Journal*, 25 February 1983.

74. On the basis of comments by participants in "Solvency, Stability and the External Debt of Developing Countries," conference sponsored by the University of Chicago and the Johnson Foundation, May 27, 1983, Racine, Wisconsin.

the official channel to pressure new bank lending. The more compulsory such pressure becomes, the more claim banks will have to official compensation if losses do occur.

The second channel for enforcement of collective bank behavior is the network of influence the large banks have on smaller banks. The large banks can impose retaliatory measures such as exclusion from future syndicated loans or termination of correspondent services.

An important third channel, however, may have to be used as well: the particular debt-rescheduling technique of the country itself. As a mild measure, the debtor country might announce that banks refusing to participate in a general program of credit extension would no longer be welcome to participate in future lending to the country once more normal times return. Of course, the country can also exert pressure on banks that have branches within its borders, but such banks in most cases will already be the most avid supporters of a bank-IMF package of new lending (because their stakes in the country's future are the highest).

A more dramatic, but more risky approach would be for the debtor country to announce that it will provide less favorable treatment for banks that do not participate in an extension of exposure that is agreed upon among the country, the IMF, and the major creditor banks. For example, the country could announce that any bank refusing to participate in credit extension under such an officially blessed program would have its loans subordinated to those of the banks that did participate, meaning that in the event of future breakdown in the process the nonparticipating banks would be the last to redeem their exposure. Announcement of loan subordination could involve risk of general erosion of confidence, however. It would probably be a measure for which the country would want to secure official (IMF, central bank) and large-bank support before implementation, in order that adverse psychological effects (even on large banks) not overwhelm the incentive effects for small bank cooperation.

It should be noted that to some extent the approach of loan subordination is already being applied informally as there is at least some indication that certain countries in arrears are allowing them to accumulate primarily on loans held by banks not carrying out their part of a generally agreed bank strategy of new lending.[75] It is also important to recognize that a more formal process of loan subordination probably could be challenged legally because of cross-default clauses in syndicated loan agreements, whereby all participants

---

75. *Washington Post*, 29 April 1983.

agree to call the borrower in default if one participant does so. On the other hand, because the legal basis for such clauses rests on the concept of mutual cooperation to secure repayment, it could be argued by the large banks that small banks calling for default did not warrant fulfillment of cross-default commitments because such smaller banks had violated the spirit of mutual action on behalf of repayment by their prior unwillingness to bear their fair share of the coordinated new lending.

By coordinated pressure through these three channels of action—official (IMF and central bank), large bank, and debtor country—it may be possible largely to overcome the free-rider problem and to achieve for private banks as a group the basic results indicated by the simple monopoly-bank model of involuntary lending.

Policy Implications of Involuntary Lending

The analysis of involuntary lending has major implications for policy on developing-country debt. As table 18 suggests, there is a wide range over which banks can be expected to keep lending new money to shore up the security of the old money. This dynamic is crucial because continued bank lending will be essential if the programs for the major debtors are to hold together; the amounts required are too large for the official community to carry without participation by the banks.

A second essential conclusion is that it is important to ensure the dynamics of this lending process by marshalling support from smaller banks that otherwise might try to enjoy a free ride by remaining out of any extension of new credit (while benefiting from the maintenance of the security of their own past loans afforded by the new contributions of the major banks and public sources). Pressure should be brought at three levels to ensure this cooperation: official, bank to bank, and debtor country. In particular, debtor countries might do well to announce that the outstanding debt of uncooperative banks will be subordinated, although this step should only be taken after close consultation with larger banks and public officials in industrial countries.

Finally, a perhaps surprising implication of this analysis is that it would be a mistake to take banks ''off the hook'' by having an international agency buy up their claims on developing countries. By so doing, public policy would choke off the most important source of new lending for countries in difficulty: involuntary bank lending. With their claims shifted from the country to an international agency, the banks would no longer have an incentive to provide new loans to the country. The benefit of the new loans constituted by reduced probability of default *times* outstanding debt would no longer enter their calculations. This adverse effect on new bank lending is a central reason why several newly proposed schemes for international debt relief would not appear to be desirable (section 7).

The broad conclusion of this analysis of involuntary lending is relatively sanguine: with proper policy measures for enforcement of cooperation among smaller banks (to avoid the free-rider problem), it should be possible to keep enough new bank lending moving to tide over illiquid major borrowers until recovery of the international economy permits them to return to capital markets on a basis of voluntary lending.

Rescheduling Techniques

Debt rescheduling is at once an admission of debt-servicing breakdown and a remedial measure for reestablishing more normal financial conditions. It is important that the design of rescheduling arrangements be as expert as possible, to avoid subsequent financial disruptions attributable to technical miscalculations.

The rescheduling of official debt has traditionally taken place in "Paris Club" meetings of donor countries. For the major debtors whose debt bulks large in international bank exposure, however, reschedulings of debt owed to private banks are more important. In the past ad hoc meetings of banks (usually in London) have drawn up these reschedulings. In the major episodes for Mexico, Brazil, and Argentina, rescheduling of bank debt has been orchestrated by the IMF, as described in section 2. The discussion here focuses on the technical structure of these reschedulings.

One issue in rescheduling is the interest rate on rescheduled debt, and the rescheduling fee. There has been considerable outcry (and even self-doubts among bankers) against the typically high interest rates on rescheduled debt and rescheduling fees.[76] Some argue that these charges reduce the chances that the country can regain its economic health. And the US bank regulators, in response to congressional pressure, have proposed that rescheduling fees (and lending fees generally) be taken as income over the life of the loan

---

76. Caroline Atkinson and James L. Rowe, Jr., "Debt Terms: Medicine Worse than Disease?" *Washington Post*, 19 June 1983.

rather than reported as income fully received in the year of rescheduling—thereby avoiding overstatement of the profitability of rescheduled loans.[77]

Amortization of rescheduling fees is largely a symbolic issue because the amounts involved are small. The higher interest rates on rescheduled loans are much more important. For example, average interest paid by Mexico on new borrowing in 1978–80 was a spread of 0.9 percentage points above LIBOR; but on its loans rescheduled in 1982 Mexico agreed to pay a spread of 1⅞ percentage points (and on its new borrowings it agreed to a spread of 2½ percentage points).[78]

Interest increases of these magnitudes do not seem particularly excessive under the circumstances. Considering the model of involuntary lending, the credit market is not really "clearing"; instead, credit rationing is taking place at an essentially negotiated interest rate. A higher interest rate partly compensates for increased risk to the lender. A higher rate also serves the positive function of discouraging unnecessary rescheduling attempts—there should be some penalty for rescheduling, although how much is an open question.

More importantly, higher interest rates contribute to the incentive of lenders to continue lending. For larger lenders, the dynamics of involuntary lending (section 4) mean that they are locked in and the interest rate is to some extent arbitrary, as long as it is no lower than the rate on the original loan. But, as discussed above, incentives are clearly needed to induce the smaller lenders to increase their exposure, and for them a higher interest rate on rescheduled loans can be an important factor in going along with an entire debt rescheduling program that includes new loans.

Moreover, the profit impact of an increased spread is much greater than the cost impact for the borrower. In the Mexican example, an increased spread from 0.9 percentage points to 1.87 percentage points doubles the profit potential to the lender, as represented by the spread above LIBOR, considering that the lender is highly leveraged and lending on the basis of borrowed funds.

---

77. Federal Reserve Board of Governors, FDIC, and Comptroller of the Currency, "Joint Memorandum: Program for Improved Supervision and Regulation of International Lending" (Washington: April 7, 1983; processed).

78. World Bank, *Annual Report 1980* (Washington, 1980), p. 148, and House of Commons, Fourth Report from the Treasury and Civil Service Committee, *International Monetary Arrangements: International Lending by Banks*, vol. 1 (March 15, 1983), p. xxviii.

In contrast, for the borrower such an increase raises interest costs only by 8 percent if LIBOR is 10 percentage points. (That is, .9/10.9 = .08.) At the same time, it would be awkward, if not impossible, to establish two classes of interest rates: a lower level for large banks locked into new lending and a higher level for small banks that require convincing.

In short, some increase in the interest rate on rescheduled loans (and new lending) is probably a sensible market response to the situation, and helps mobilize further lending at a reasonable additional cost to the borrower. The crucial issue is mobilization of funds rather than limited changes in their price. In any event the borrower can prepay the loans and replace them with others at lower rates if the country enjoys a surge in its external performance and creditworthiness, and market rates decline (as has happened in the past). Nonetheless, the political response of borrowing countries to higher spreads appears to be potentially acrimonious, and considering that the rate is to some extent arbitrary, there may be some room for smaller increases of interest rates on rescheduled loans than recently applied. Indeed, congressional ire at seeming bank exploitation led to a provision in the House-approved version of the bill to increase IMF quotas, prohibiting "any fee exceeding the administrative cost of the restructuring."[79] That restriction goes too far, however, if the problem of mobilizing lending from the smaller banks is taken into account.

A second major aspect of rescheduling concerns coverage. Mexico and Brazil represent sharply different alternatives. Mexico rescheduled all of its public debt owed to banks due from August 1982 through December 1984, including short-term debt, for a total of approximately $20 billion. In contrast, Brazil rescheduled only $4 billion in long-term bank debt coming due in 1983.[80]

Brazil consciously sought to minimize formal rescheduling—for fear of its impact on later creditworthiness—and relied heavily on moral suasion to avoid a decline in outstanding short-term credit. Brazilian authorities also considered their underlying situation to be stronger than Mexico's and apparently felt they could return to the capital market on a voluntary basis later in 1983. The strategy for Brazil, developed with the cooperation of the IMF and private banks, included a four-part program for bank loans: Project 1 involved $4.4 billion in new loans for 1983; Project 2, rescheduling of $4

79. US Congress, House Committee on Banking, Finance, and Urban Affairs, *International Recovery and Financial Stability Act*, H.R. 2957, sec. 319 (a)(1), 98 Cong., 1st sess., 1983.

80. House of Commons, *International Monetary Arrangements*, and *Wall Street Journal*, 10 February 1983.

billion in long-term debt coming due; under Project 3, banks were to keep open short-term trade-credit lines of approximately $9 billion; and in Project 4, banks were to restore short-term interbank deposits in foreign branches of Brazilian banks to $7.5 billion (82 percent of their June 30, 1982 level). But Project 4 failed seriously, because many European banks in particular failed to meet this commitment, and this component of the package remained approximately $1.5 billion short, contributing to growing arrears of nearly $1 billion by mid-1983. Part of the problem was that some European central banks (especially the Swiss) opposed the use of overnight interbank funds for long-term lending. Another element of the problem was that the interest spreads on interbank deposits are much lower than on new lending, giving little incentive to maintain these deposits.[81]

The lesson of the Brazilian and Mexican packages would seem to be that, in the absence of very strong reasons to believe that moral suasion can keep up short-term credit lines, it is better to have a more complete rescheduling (and longer—Mexico's is for two years' principal) than to rely on voluntary maintenance of credit lines combined with a smaller amount of rescheduling. Part of the problem is that Brazil's underlying economic situation did show substantial erosion in 1982 because of low exports, and only under strong fundamentals would a voluntary, market-oriented response, combined with only a limited amount of rescheduling, have much prospect of success.[82] Another lesson is that the interbank market is the least reliable of all as a source of credit-line maintenance.

Whether to reschedule a single year's debt coming due or to reschedule several years' debt is another technical issue. The major rescheduling cases have involved restructuring of the principal due, to be repaid over seven or eight years with two to four years' grace period. These reschedulings have been either for one year's principal (Brazil, Argentina, Ecuador, Peru) or two years' principal (Mexico, Chile).[83] The question arises as to whether it would be advisable to restructure debt for three or even more years. The

---

81. *Wall Street Journal*, 24 February 1983; *Financial Times*, 31 May 1983.

82. In this regard the contrast between Yugoslavia and Brazil is informative. The Yugoslav package involves debt rollover of both short- and long-term debt, rather than formal rescheduling. However, with a net debt to exports ratio of only 114 percent in 1982 compared with Brazil's 382 percent (section 3), Yugoslavia was in a stronger fundamental position.

83. House of Commons, Fourth Report from the Treasury and Civil Service Committee, sess. 1982–83, *International Monetary Arrangements: International Lending by Banks*, vol. 1 (March 15, 1983), pp. xxviii-ix.

classic issue in rescheduling duration is the choice between keeping lender leverage by keeping the country on a "short leash," on the one hand, and providing a longer term planning horizon for the country, on the other. Once again, the contrast between the initial experience of Mexico and Brazil suggests that at least two-year reschedulings establish better conditions for orderly adjustment than single-year reschedulings. Given the problems Brazil has had in 1983, negotiations for a 1984 rescheduling could prove difficult. Indeed, if an interim breakdown were to occur in the Brazilian package, the chances are good that Brazil would leapfrog the Mexican model and request a multiyear rescheduling of perhaps three years.

Treatment of private debt is another difficult point in rescheduling. Private debt has especially caused problems. In Mexico even interest on private debt was not paid for several months. In Mexico, Venezuela, and to some exent Argentina, the model emerging for private debt has been that the debtor country's government would promise a desirable exchange rate for its repayment only if the creditors would reschedule, facing creditors with the choice of providing rescheduling or seeing their private debtors go bankrupt.[84] This strategy appears to have succeeded but at the cost of considerable frustration on the part of the creditor banks. In the case of Chile, conflict over private debt was substantial. Private debt is high, accounting for approximately 60 percent of Chilean external debt.[85] Credit cutoffs occurred after the government liquidated several large domestic banks and refused to guarantee their external debts. In subsequent negotiations foreign banks insisted that the Chilean government assume responsibility for all private debt; eventually the government agreed to do so only for the debts of Chilean banks, not other private firms.[86]

Although there is no simple solution to treatment of private debt, in the rescheduling process private debt should be more systematically integrated into the total package. At the same time, foreign creditors can hardly expect governments to grant ex post guarantees of loans extended on the basis of private risk; nor can governments completely wash their hands of these loans, considering that there was at least an implicit contract that foreign exchange would be available to permit their servicing. This implicit responsibility is especially relevant where the governments' own policies encourage rapid

---

84. See, for example, *Financial Times*, 8 April 1983.

85. *Ercilla* (Chile), 2 February 1983, p. 14.

86. *Washington Post*, 6 May 1983, and discussions with Chilean experts.

debt build-up, even if its form was private. In short, private debt should be included as a significant part of the debt renegotiation process in a more systematic manner than in the major recent cases.

To recapitulate, there are technical questions about the best type of rescheduling once debt rescheduling becomes necessary. The evidence of 1982–83 suggests that interest rates on rescheduled debt may have to be increased above original levels to facilitate the process of involuntary lending, although because of political reaction in borrowing countries it may be prudent to limit such increases to modest amounts; that, unless the borrower is truly in a strong fundamental position, formal rescheduling is preferable to disguised, quasi-voluntary rescheduling—especially through the device of maintenance of interbank credit lines; that rescheduling of two years is probably preferable to one, although rescheduling of much longer periods might involve excessive loss of lender leverage; and that private debt should be more formally integrated into the rescheduling process.

Default Incentives

Along the continuum of debt disruptions, the most severe are outright repudiation and extended, unilateral, complete moratorium (indefinite suspension of payment of both principal and interest). These two forms of debt disruption may appropriately be called "default," a term often used rather inappropriately to include even temporary payments disruptions and reschedulings. Because of the growing apprehension that some debtor nations might find adjustment programs too onerous to fulfill and might, instead, declare an extended moratorium, it is important to consider the possible incentives and disincentives to default.

In a classic article, Martin Bronfenbrenner argued that a nation would have an incentive to expropriate foreign investment once the sum total of expected future inflows of new investment (appropriately discounted by an interest rate) became smaller than the value of existing investment.[87] More recent theoretical work has emphasized the utilty of foreign borrowing to smooth out fluctuations in consumption (for example, because of commodity price fluctuations). This benefit from borrowing enters in the trade-off involved between the attraction of defaulting (to discard the debt burden) on

---

87. Martin Bronfenbrenner, "The Appeal of Confiscation in Economic Development," *Economic Development and Cultural Change*, vol. 3 (April 1955), pp. 201–18.

TABLE 19 **Relationship of interest burden to new borrowing, nonoil developing countries**
(billion dollars)

Year	Total debt (A)	New borrowing, net[a] (B)	Interest payments (C)	Ratio, C/B (D)	Ratio, interest/new borrowing: Argentina	Brazil	Mexico	Chile
1974	160.8	. . .	9.3	. . .	0.27	0.29	0.19	0.40
1975	190.8	30.0	10.5	0.35	−4.06[b]	0.42	0.27	0.92
1976	228.0	37.2	10.9	0.29	1.27	0.39	0.34	−2.41[b]
1977	278.5	50.5	13.6	0.27	0.36	0.37	0.38	1.03
1978	336.3	57.8	19.4	0.34	0.25	0.25	0.39	0.32
1979	396.9	60.6	28.0	0.46	0.18	0.58	0.52	0.44
1980	474.0	77.1	40.4	0.52	0.27	0.86	0.42	0.45
1981	555.0	81.0	55.1	0.68	0.41	1.08	0.62	0.45
1982	612.4	57.4	59.2	1.03	2.20	0.93	0.79	0.79

Source: IMF, World Economic Outlook, 1983, pp. 200–204 and Institute for International Economics debt data base.
a. Equals debt in year minus debt in previous year.
b. Year in which debt declined.

one hand and the cost of thereby being cut off from foreign capital markets into the indefinite future, on the other.[88] In practice the decision about default goes further: it involves considerable risk that even normal trade patterns would be disrupted, beyond denial of access to the capital markets.

Considering the Bronfenbrenner dynamic, there is some cause for concern about growing incentive to default. Several important debtor countries have passed from an early stage in the debt cycle, where interest payments are small relative to new borrowing, to a late phase, where interest payments are large relative to new borrowing or even exceed it. Indeed, this transition may have been largely completed in the aggregate. As shown in table 19, for the nonoil developing countries the ratio of interest payments to net new borrowing (from all sources) rose from an average of 30 percent in 1975–78 to 55 percent in 1979–81 and 103 percent in 1982, when interest payments actually exceeded new borrowing. Similar trends are shown for four major

88. Jonathan Eaton and Mark Gersowitz, "Debt with Potential Repudiation: Theoretical and Empirical Analysis," Review of Economic Studies, vol. 48 (1981), pp. 289–309.

Latin American debtor countries.[89] The implication of this trend is that the incentive for adherence to the normal rules of international lending has been decreasing because increasingly any cutoff of new lending would be offset by termination of interest payments if developing countries chose to default.

Moreover, the rather extreme relationship of interest to new borrowing in 1982 is likely to continue over the next several years. This point may be seen intuitively by considering that debt is unlikely to continue to grow by a rate higher than the average interest rate on past debt (with LIBOR on the order of 10 percent) because of contracted capital markets. Thus, the magnitude of new debt is likely to equal or fall short of the magnitude of interest payments. The point is also evident in the simulations of section 3. As shown in the appendix table B-3 for the 19 largest debtor countries interest payments are projected to be approximately the same size as new net borrowing in 1983–86, and for the oil-importing countries interest would substantially exceed new borrowing. In short, there is an underlying structural vulnerability in international lending at the present time because, if a judgment is made solely on the basis of simple comparison of the interest burden against net new loans received, the developing countries have little incentive to continue honoring debt-servicing obligations. That is, if they defaulted, their losses in net new loans forgone would approximately equal their gains in interest relief.

In practice, however, the consequences of default could reach far beyond trading the loss of new borrowing in exchange for avoiding interest payments. A defaulting country would risk isolating itself economically from the rest of the world. At best it would forfeit the opportunity to borrow at some future date when foreign capital might be extremely vital to it, because of an export collapse, for example. In addition, even short-term trade credit could dry up, making it impossible for the country to conduct foreign trade at anywhere near normal levels. The denial of short-term trade credits would mean that the country would have to go to a cash basis for its imports. In order to do this it would have to have reserves worth perhaps six months of imports. That is, although in principle a country could continue trade without normal trade credits, it would have to pay cash for imports, and because of the lag in export receipts behind shipments, it would have to expect to wait

---

89. For 1983 the relationships are even more drastic in Brazil and Mexico. Their adjustment programs call, respectively, for current account deficits (i.e., a figure that *exceeds* new borrowing in the form of loans, considering that some direct foreign investment will be received) of $3.4 billion and $6.9 billion, respectively; by contrast, their interest burdens are projected at approximately $11 billion each.

a number of months between the shipment of exports and the availability of their earnings for spending on imports. In short, only countries with large reserves could continue trade on a cash basis. Ironically, these would be precisely the countries that would not be in serious debt difficulty in the first place.

Beyond difficulties with access to long-term and short-term credit, defaulting countries could face reprisals. Foreign creditors could attach any of the foreign assets of a defaulting country, as well as its exports abroad (commercial airlines, ships, bank accounts, shipments of commodities, and so forth). For example, in 1972 Kennecott Copper Corporation successfully obtained legal seizure of Chilean copper shipments at a French port, as well as the freezing of Chilean bank accounts in New York, because Kennecott maintained that Salvador Allende had paid inadequate compensation for its expropriated copper mine.[90] Parallel actions could certainly be expected against countries defaulting on external debt. Notably, the only two countries to repudiate debt in recent decades—Cuba in 1961 and North Korea in 1974—did so under conditions that seriously impaired their access to Western (especially US) financial markets.

There is, of course, a wide range of uncertainty about the nature of such international responses. Along the continuum of debt disruption, it is conceivable that if such important countries as Brazil and Mexico declared an indefinite moratorium for reasons of inability to pay, the US government would make no attempt to take reprisals, because of the desire to avoid more permanent jeopardy to political ties. Even in this more benign version of moratorium, however, private parties would have legal access to the type of attachments and interdictions just described, and it would be unlikely that Western governments would actively block the private actors in these efforts. To be sure, in this event the private concerns with truly large interests (especially the major banks) would first seek to reestablish a payment schedule through negotiation before attempting to attach assets, because any assets they could attach would be small relative to their claims on the country. But in the event of extended inability to reestablish negotiations, these private concerns might eventually join in the action of other private creditors to seize assets and shipments.

Under more aggressive circumstances, moreover, such as a moratorium declaration coupled with internal government changes moving significantly to the left (or to the nationalist-right) and announced in terms laying the

---

90. *New York Times*, 5 October 1972.

blame on Western nations, international official reaction might reinforce private reprisals. At the extreme, Western nations might impose trade embargoes on the defaulting country. Such a step would complete the process of moving toward autarky that the country would risk when it first decided on an extended moratorium.

The possibility of international reprisal explains the superficial appeal of the idea of a debtors' cartel. It would be more difficult for industrial countries to impose reprisals such as asset attachments and trade sanctions on a wide coalition of debtor countries taking joint action. A debtors' cartel would be a political coalition to ward off reprisals rather than a traditional economic cartel regulating the supply of a product. The appeal of such a cartel is greatest to the smaller countries and to the less creditworthy countries. If they could enroll large debtors into a common front, small countries seeking to default could greatly reduce the likelihood of foreign reprisals against themselves. Not surprisingly, however, such a cartel has held little appeal for the large debtor countries, even after the sharp deteriorations in their credit positions. They have no desire to tarnish their long-term credit standings further by declaring a common front with certain smaller countries with even more severe debt problems. The very formation of a debtors' cartel would be equivalent to signaling creditors that they could expect aggressive behavior in the future, thereby cutting back even further the availability of new voluntary lending now and in the medium-term future.

On the contrary, there is a strong incentive for individual debtors to attempt to maintain their credit image on a basis of their individual performance. In the late 1970s major borrowers were systematically resistant to calls for general debt relief in the context of North-South negotiations, because they did not want to see their own credit ratings jeopardized. And in late 1982 Brazilian authorities went to great lengths to disassociate themselves from the Mexican financial crisis, maintaining that Brazilian policies had been more prudent. Ironically, by mid-1983 Mexico's adjustment was proceeding more smoothly than Brazil's, and correspondingly Mexico had no desire to be judged on the credit merits of any other Latin American country than itself.

The dynamic of credit-rating self preservation seems likely to defeat attempts to establish a debtors' cartel. Indeed, the major debtors repeatedly have rejected such proposals. Moreover, the dynamic of individual credit-rating preservation also means that it is by no means axiomatic that if a major debtor such as Brazil or Mexico were to default, or to insist on extreme measures such as interest rescheduling, all other debtor countries would demand the same treatment. Some of the weakest debtors might do so, but other more important debtors very probably would find such an event the occasion to make it clear to creditors that they themselves could be trusted to honor their obligations and were by comparison preferred credit risks. In this way the nondefaulting debtors could not only avoid unnecessary risks of foreign reprisal but would also buttress their future ability to borrow. For all these reasons, an emergence of a meaningful debtors' cartel is unlikely.

In short, the dramatic potential costs of default mean that even if interest somewhat exceeds new borrowing, countries are unlikely to judge it beneficial on balance to default. Moreover, debtors are unlikely to form a cartel and carry out a joint default. Instead, it is much more likely that if normal rescheduling breaks down, a country will go into protracted negotiations, seeking to obtain the equivalent of relief from full market terms on its debt, but in a form that does not proclaim default. Nicaragua is one of the few illustrations. In part because it was in a postwar reconstruction, the new Sandinista regime managed in 1980 to get foreign banks to reschedule not only principal but also all interest in excess of 7 percent. At the present time, the Polish case also represents an attempt in this direction. In mid-1983 the Polish government stated (as a negotiating position) that it wished to reschedule its entire $25 billion debt to the West over 20 years, with an eight-year period during which no interest would be paid.[91] In both cases, the rescheduling of interest is an extreme step for banks to accept, because it invites the possibility of eventual nonpayment of interest (and, importantly, the failure to pay interest within a specified period of the date due triggers classification of the loan as nonperforming on the banks' books). In the Polish case, acceptance of the proposed terms would push the country further in the direction of de facto default. In this context, it is perhaps not an accident that both Nicaragua and Poland are in political situations that tend to reduce the likelihood of future capital inflows from the United States and some other industrial countries, echoing the political isolation of the former default countries, Cuba and North Korea.

A more significant threat to Western banks than outright default, then, is that some developing countries may seek to obtain reschedulings that substantially depart from normal market terms. The first departure would be rescheduling of interest as well as principal. A more radical departure would be the negotiation of below-market interest rates on rescheduled debt.

At the present time even this kind of "radical rescheduling" seems

91. "Polish Officials Seek to Reschedule Debt," *Washington Post*, 15 June 1983.

unlikely, because it would seriously damage the country's long-term credit standing. But if world recession were to continue and developing-country export performance remained stagnant, the pressures for this kind of solution would mount. Moreover, considering the high degree of bank vulnerability to developing-country debt, the large debtor countries would appear to have substantial unexploited bargaining potential. If negotiations moved from a cooperative to a confrontational mode, large borrowers might be able to extract substantial debt relief as a bribe or side-payment to keep them from defaulting in a context where there would be some costs to themselves but much greater costs to the creditors and the financial system. (Thus, potentially the amount of "rent" or side-payment they could extract would be the difference between these two costs.) So far, however, the major debtors remain cooperative. Considering the structural weakness of their incentive to continue playing by the rules (with interest exceeding new loans) and their great potential bargaining leverage in view of the heavy exposure of bank capital that they hold, it is to the credit of the long-range judgment of the financial leadership of these countries that they have not yet moved to an adversarial posture relative to the banks nor sought to exploit their bargaining potential in the form of radical reschedulings on nonmarket terms. How long this prudence, and willingness to play by established rules, will continue will undoubtedly depend on whether their economic situations deteriorate further, and by how much.

In sum, despite structural trends that specifically raise the incentives to default, the major debtor countries (except perhaps Poland) still remain far from the point where default or radical rescheduling on nonmarket terms would be an attractive option.

5   Adequacy of Banking Institutions

The external debt disruptions of 1982–83 have raised new doubts about the adequacy of present banking arrangements. In particular, in considering whether to approve increased IMF quotas, many legislators have objected that higher quotas would be a bailout for the banks, and that the banks got themselves into difficulty through excessive and irresponsible lending abroad.[92]

---

92. For a statement of this viewpoint, see *Wall Street Journal*, editorial, 9 March 1983.

The result of this wave of criticism of bank behavior has been congressional pressure for tighter regulation of banks, and a response by the regulatory authorities proposing somewhat heightened regulation of external lending. At the same time, many academic critics have questioned whether the organization of central bank responsibility for the "lender-of-last-resort" function has been adequate for international lending.

This section first examines whether there are structural flaws in the organization of international bank lending that led to debt crises. It then reviews the proposals for new regulation of external loans. The discussion concludes with an examination of the argument that central bank coverage of international lending is inadequate, thereby posing a risk to the system.

Organization of Foreign Lending

Many critics hold that in the 1970s bank lending to developing countries was excessive, and that it departed from past standards of prudence.[93] However, as was widely recognized in the mid-1970s and again in 1979–80, bank lending played a socially valuable role in facilitating the financial recycling of OPEC surpluses to nonoil developing countries in the process of adjustment.[94] Official lending responded only sluggishly, especially to middle-income countries, so that it was primarily bank lending that met the sharply increased need for financing. Moreover, as was repeatedly pointed out at the time, if this lending had not been forthcoming, developing countries would have been forced to cut back their imports from industrial countries, causing an even sharper world recession after the first oil shock.[95]

---

93. See, for example, David Lomax, "Sovereign Risk Analysis Now," *The Banker* (January 1983), pp. 33–39.

94. Although it would be wrong to imply, as has often been done, that developing-country deficits were largely caused by OPEC surpluses. In a statistical examination I have found that from 1973–81 a change in the OPEC surplus by a given magnitude translated into a corresponding change only 14 percent as large in the deficits of nonoil developing countries, and that in addition the developing countries had a high ongoing deficit as well as a sharp response in their deficits to changes in OECD growth. William R. Cline, "External Debt: System Vulnerability and Development," *Columbia Journal of World Business*, vol. 17, no. 1 (Spring 1982), pp. 4–14.

95. John A. Holson and Jean L. Waelbroeck, "The Less Developed Countries and the International Monetary Mechanism," *American Economic Review*, vol. 66, no. 2 (May 1976), pp. 171–76.

There were of course market forces inducing heightened bank lending abroad. As was recognized by international agencies, both the surge of deposits "from oil exporters surpluses" and the "dampening effect of the international recession on competing demands for bank loans in the industrial countries" caused an expansion in the supply of bank lending to developing countries.[96] It should be added that the innovation of variable interest loans greatly contributed to bank willingness to lend in an inflationary environment.

In short, a substantial rise in the relative magnitude of bank lending to developing countries in the 1970s was not only to be expected from international macroeconomic developments, but was also broadly socially desirable. Nonetheless, by the late 1970s and early 1980s many qualified observers questioned whether the dynamic response of banks had become too much of a good thing. Henry C. Wallich of the Federal Reserve Board of Governors criticized the growth of bank lending to developing countries as unsustainably rapid, and at an average pace of 25 percent from 1975 to 1980 it was rapid indeed.[97]

After the rash of debt disruptions in 1982–83 it became fashionable, especially among conservative-populists to charge that banks had acted irresponsibly. The demonstration in section 1 of this study that international economic forces contributed extremely large amounts to indebtedness, especially in 1980–82, should be sufficient evidence to dispel the notion that bank irresponsibility, and for that matter, country irresponsibility, has been the sole or primary cause of today's debt problem. Nonetheless, it is important to consider whether flaws exist in the organization of international bank lending that have contributed to the problem.

In 1979 I suggested, based on the Peruvian experience, that banks might be lending excessively because they tended to assume that international institutions and OECD governments would come to the country's aid in case of trouble, and that banks thereby "externalized" the risk in foreign lending.[98] While any such bias toward excess lending surely could not account for the bulk of increased developing-country debt in recent years (again, considering the large external shocks in recent years enumerated in section 1), this

---

96. IMF *Annual Report* (Washington, 1976), p. 21.

97. Henry C. Wallich. "Banks, LDC's Share Concern For Viable System," *Journal of Commerce,* 30 July 1981, p. 4A; and BIS *Annual Report* (Basle, 1978), p. 92 and 1981, p. 105.

98. William R. Cline and Sidney Weintraub, eds., *Economic Stabilization in Developing Countries*, pp. 40–41.

influence may nonetheless be a factor to address. Similarly, in the late 1970s, the desire of European, Japanese, and regional US banks to enter more actively into international lending appears to have contributed to increased lending supply at low spreads above LIBOR as new and traditional lenders competed for market shares.[99]

These various supply factors, including ample availability of funds from OPEC deposits, in some important cases led to continued bank lending to countries that ideally would have borrowed less while adopting adjustment measures under IMF auspices but instead availed themselves of bank financing. A conspicuous case was Peru in 1976; Mexico and Argentina in 1981 to early 1982 also would fit this description. Thus, from December 1981 to June 1982 when Mexico was in the last phase of budgetary and other policy excess before its August crisis, US banks increased their exposure in Mexico at an annual rate of 34 percent. And from December 1979 to December 1980, as Argentina pursued a policy of extreme overvaluation, US banks increased their exposure in Argentina by 42 percent.[100]

The experience of international lending in the last decade suggests a need for better discipline and organization of bank lending. There is a need not only to avoid excessive lending, and some excessive lending undoubtedly did occur in the 1970s, but also to avoid severe cutbacks in lending, such as occurred in 1982. Some analysts have advocated that the International Monetary Fund formally adopt the role of mentor to bank lending, and that it provide a "traffic signal" showing a green light for lending to countries pursuing desirable policies but an amber or red light warning against bank lending to countries not doing so. Indeed, the IMF already acts as a moderator in the other direction: as outlined above, it has pressed banks to combine new lending in countries where they might otherwise hold back and undermine a financial recovery package.

An IMF traffic signal would involve difficult political problems. Intense lobbying of the more powerful members would accompany any case where an amber or red light was about to be activated. Yet if the IMF had officially maintained a green light for a country that subsequently had debt difficulties,

---

99. Thus, the average spread above LIBOR for Eurocurrency loans to developing countries was about 1 percentage point in 1973–74, 1.5 percent in 1975–77, down to 1.2 percent again by 1978, and only 0.9 percent in 1979–81. IMF *International Capital Markets, Recent Developments and Short-term Prospects,* September 1980, p. 26, and July 1982, p. 15.

100. Federal Financial Institutions Examination Council, *Country Exposure Lending Survey,* various issues.

at the least official credibility would be undermined and at the most banks might claim official responsibility for their difficulties.

A more promising vehicle for improving the organization of bank lending is the new Institute for International Finance (IIF). This organization, formed by international private banks, has as its primary mandate the provision of improved information about borrowing countries. The "information gap" hypothesis holds that a major contributing factor in the debt crises of 1982 was that individual banks did not know how rapidly their competitors were expanding lending, especially short-term, and that by the time the true magnitude of increased debt was known the situation was out of control. Although this view surely overstates the role of information per se, a better information system could make a modest contribution, especially because the central source of data on bank exposure—the bank for International Settlements—provides this data only after a six-month lag.

The Institute for International Finance has a much more important potential agenda, however, if its members (and antitrust lawyers) allow it to pursue one. It could evaluate country borrowers, and ideally, assign them credit ratings. Existing private rating firms are paid by the countries (or firms) they rate, and countries tend not to finance a rating unless it is likely to come out favorably. A country-rating mechanism by private banks would avoid the drawbacks of imposing an official straight jacket on the market. It could of course be subject to bias from banks with existing exposure in a given country, although it might be possible to design sufficient staff independence that such bias could be minimized (for example, through liaison with international agencies).

The Institute for International Finance could also help moderate downswings in capital flows by assisting in the mobilization of lending support from otherwise free-riding banks (section 4).

In sum, although it is inaccurate to attribute the debt problem chiefly to past bank irresponsibility, the experience of the last decade has shown the need for bringing more order to bank lending so that it does not swing from excessive expansion to excessive contraction. The Institute for International Finance could play an important institutional role (well beyond merely providing information) in addressing the problem of organizing international lending. Some analysts have expressed concern that any such institutional change could have adverse effects on developing countries through the cartelization of credit markets.[101] But at least in the medium term, following

---

101. Edmar L. Bacha and Carlos Diaz-Alejandro, "International Financial Intermediation: A Long and Tropical View," *Princeton Essays In International Finance,* no. 147 (Princeton, NJ: International Finance Section, Department of Economics, Princeton University, May 1982).

the events of 1982–83, it is likely that a more organized credit market would increase the supply of credit rather than restrict supply in classic cartel fashion.[102]

Bank Regulation

Beyond institutional innovation in the private market, the official regulators are also moving to introduce more discipline in foreign lending, in part because of congressional pressure on them to do so as a quid pro quo for increased IMF quotas (in view of the political argument against bailing out banks).

It is important to recognize that tightened bank regulation will not solve any immediate problem; at the moment the problem is too little new bank lending to developing countries, not too much. Nonetheless, it would be imprudent to delay longer in taking necessary steps to strengthen the system for the long run.

The basic problem regulatory reform needs to address is the overextension of sovereign lending beyond limits that are prudent for the system. The system now appears too vulnerable to loans extended to developing and East European countries, as illustrated by the loan-capital ratios and default scenarios examined in section 2. Similarly, it appears that at present the US system seems to have generated relatively modest provisioning, or setting aside of reserves, for loans to countries in difficulty. Thus, in 1982 the nine largest US banks had an estimated total provisioning of $614 million attributable to foreign loans, or about 1.7 percent of the value of their total loans outstanding to countries that have experienced significant debt disruption recently.[103] Although provisioning means short-run nuisance in lower reported

---

102. Moreover, the lending market is so competitive that achievement of a cartel that could extract monopoly rent would be highly unlikely, quite apart from antitrust enforcement.

103. The provisioning figure is based on the banks' annual reports. The total loans referred to amounted to $36.7 billion for 11 countries (Argentina, Brazil, Chile, Costa Rica, Mexico, Nicaragua, Peru, Sudan, Zaire, Poland, and Romania). Federal Financial Institutions Examination Council, "Country Exposure Lending Survey: December 1982" (Washington, 1983; processed). However, capital positions have been improving. The 17 largest banks raised their capital-to-loan ratio from 4.39 percent at the end of 1980 to 5.02 percent at the end of 1982. Communication with Federal Reserve staff, April 1983.

profits, inadequate provisioning risks shock to international banks and the system under unfavorable scenarios.

The Federal Reserve, Comptroller of the Currency, and Federal Deposit Insurance Corporation have explicitly recognized the "transfer" risk in sovereign lending caused by the possible inability of a country to raise enough foreign exchange to service debt.[104] This recognition is important in itself, because in the past some prominent bankers have asserted that sovereign lending has no risk at all because countries do not disappear. The three agencies have proposed a five-point program of regulation. It involves (a) a stricter examination of country exposure, including expectation of higher capital-to-loan ratios for banks with greater concentration of country exposure; (b) more public disclosure of the country exposure of banks; (c) the definition of new loan classifications: Loss, Reservable, and Debt-Service Impaired, with requirements for write-off or provisioning into reserves in the first two cases, respectively; (d) stretchout of reported income from loan fees; and (e) increased cooperation with bank regulators abroad and, possibly, greater sharing of IMF information.

These proposals are highly desirable reforms. They generally strike the proper balance between sufficient reform to increase prudence in the system and avoidance of overkill that would cut off foreign lending. They may tend to err in the direction of leniency by not requiring any loan provisioning for rescheduled loans as long as the new terms of the loans are met. Under this approach there would be no required provisioning of loans to Mexico and Brazil currently, and would have been none for Poland in 1981 or 1982, even though in some countries with more conservative banking practice (for example, Switzerland) considerable provisioning has been taking place for these countries (although typically with encouragement, rather than require-ment, by central banks). Unfortunately, however, the application of normal provisioning rates (10 to 15 percent of face value annually, up to an eventual 50 percent) would be far in excess of the amount needed for rescheduled loans and would impose a severe burden on banks. Loans to countries that have rescheduled in the last year account for perhaps 150 percent of capital of the large banks, meaning that provisioning of up to 15 percent of capital annually might be required, wiping out bank profits. Such provisioning could be regulatory overkill. Thus, the recommendation of provisioning of resched-

104. Joint Memorandum: "Federal Reserve, FDIC, and Comptroller of the Currency. Program for Improved Supervision and Regulation of International Lending" (Washington, April 7, 1983; processed).

uled loans, contained in the House of Representatives version of the bill for the IMF quota increase,[105] would appear highly undesirable. If retained, provisioning of rescheduled loans should be explicitly set at a much lower level than for generally doubtful loans (for example, only 2 percent to 3 percent per year). Alternatively, it might be appropriate to provision only against that amount of principal actually postponed, rather than against the full loan.

Conceptually a challenging question is whether the reforms should include country ceilings. The joint memorandum argues that country differences, political pressures, and the current high exposure of some banks in some countries rule out country ceilings. Broadly, the position of the regulators appears correct, as discussed below. Nonetheless, it is perhaps useful to conceptionalize possible theoretical approaches to country limits.

Domestically a US bank cannot lend more than 15 percent of its capital to a single borrower, whether it is General Motors or the corner drug store. If this domestic regulation is valid, some corresponding ceiling on country loans might also follow logically.[106] Specifically, if the domestic probability of default in general is at a given level, A, and the probability of default on country loans is at another level, B, then the same logic that gives a 15 percent loan ceiling to domestic loans would imply a loan ceiling of 15 percent *times* A/B in country lending. Thus, if the probability of default by a borrowing country is one-fifth the probability of default for a domestic borrower, the country loan ceiling should be 15 percent *times* 5, or 75 percent. In that way the expected or probability-weighted damage to the bank from a single country borrower would be the same as that from a single domestic borrower. In the past some thought that the probability of country default was zero, so that conceptually the loan ceiling would be infinite (A/B = infinity, when B = 0). Today the probability of country default no longer appears to be zero. It must be kept in mind that unlike domestic loans, country loans have no tangible collateral.

In practice, there appears at present to be little firm basis for determining

---

105. US Congress, House Committee on Banking, Finance, and Urban Affairs, *International Recovery and Financial Stability Act*, H.R. 2957, 98 Cong., 1st sess., 1983.

106. The 15 percent limit does apply to a single central government, but considering state firms and private borrowers there is no corresponding country ceiling. Note, however, that there is no ceiling domestically on interrelated loans—such as loans to different oil companies—yet the interrelatedness risk bears some resemblance to transfer risk.

the risk of country as opposed to domestic default (B relative to A), making it difficult or impossible to apply the above approach operationally. One recent study concluded that the real cost to creditors of all debt rescheduling (based on the difference between original and adjusted terms on a present-value basis) between 1956 and 1980 amounted to $2 billion, compared with total loans to developing countries of $400 billion in 1980.[107] Even in the terminal year this amount was only half of 1 percent of principal, implying that over a 24-year period the average loss rate was only 0.02 percent annually. And even this loss was confined to official creditors, who had motives of concessional assistance in the cases where loss was significant (Indonesia, Ghana, India, and Pakistan). By contrast, the recognized losses on private debt reschedulings have been negligible, because reschedulings have been at market terms. To judge from past experience, then, the probability of country default B would not be far from zero and an infinite country ceiling would not be far wrong.

However, to assess country risk as zero under today's circumstances would be naive. Considering perhaps the most severe cases of country risk, loans to Poland, Zaire, and Sudan might reasonably be judged to be worth no more than two-thirds their face value. If this valuation were accepted, the implied, aggregate losses to Western banks would amount to $5.3 billion. Assuming these losses were realized over five years, and comparing them to total bank loans to developing countries and Eastern Europe, the average loss rate on country lending would be 0.28 percent annually. By comparison, for the nine largest US banks average domestic loan losses were 0.72 percent of loan value in 1982.[108] Thus, a forward-looking analysis might place the ratio A/B at approximately 260 percent, implying a country limit at approximately 40 percent of capital.

Nonetheless, the determination of the probability of country default is clearly imprecise, and in a legalistic approach it might be necessary to make the assessment of relative country default risk on actual past losses—meaning near-zero realized losses and near-infinite country ceilings. Accordingly, the

---

107. Chandra Hardy, "Rescheduling Developing-Country Debts, 1956–1980: Lessons and Recommendations," Overseas Development Council Working Paper No. 1 (Washington, February 1982), p. 26.

108. From annual reports, total loans were $398.8 billion, and domestic charge-offs were $1.4 billion in 1982. From the Federal Financial Institutions lending survey, total foreign loans were $205.3 billion. Thus, domestic loans of the nine largest banks were $193.5 billion, giving a domestic loss rate of 0.72 percent.

approach outlined above is not operational in practice, and it is probably best to accept the regulators' conclusion that establishing country ceilings would be a mistake. Pragmatically, a serious problem is that some banks have such high single-country exposure (such as Citibank with 74 percent of its capital in Brazil) that specifying a limit would either leave them in violation (and unable to bear their share of "involuntary lending") or establish an uncomfortably high limit that might lead other banks to excess. There is also the question of whether two classes of countries would have to be differentiated, with country ceilings applying to developing (and East European) but not industrial countries. Nonetheless, examination of the logic of country ceilings leaves less room for complacency about their absence today than in the past—because of the higher probability of future country default than in the past. Accordingly, the other prudential reforms proposed by the regulators are all the more welcome.

A reform that should be added to the regulators' list is more liberal income-tax treatment of reserves. It is paradoxical that at a time when the regulatory authorities seek increased provisioning, the Internal Revenue Service is attempting to reduce the share of bank loans that can be deducted when provisioned to only 0.6 percent of total loans instead of 1 percent. Surely for system stability the IRS should be making revisions in the opposite direction.

Overall, the proposals by the Federal Reserve, Comptroller of the Currency, and FDIC deserve strong support. It would be safer to adopt this strategy now, and evaluate the results in one or two years, than to risk further aggravating the liquidity problem by enacting regulatory overkill. In the longer run it is crucial to reduce bank exposure to developing countries as a fraction of bank capital. The Western financial system now is too vulnerable to developing-country debt.

Lender of Last Resort

Another area of concern about adequacy of banking institutions is that central bank "lender-of-last-resort" coverage may be inadequate for international lending. Under the traditions of central banking, a bank in difficulty borrows from its central bank if it is illiquid, although if it is insolvent the remedy involves either merger with a stronger bank or dissolution, with protection guaranteed only to insured depositors.

In international lending, however, there is ambiguity about whether the host-country central bank or that of the parent country bears the lender-of-last-resort (LLR) responsibility for a subsidiary of a foreign bank, and some observers consider this ambiguity dangerous.[109] In the case of foreign branches, there is no ambiguity: because the parent bank is legally responsible for its branches, a branch in trouble would appeal to its parent, which in turn would appeal to the parent central bank.

For subsidiaries, some confusion has existed because major central banks have agreed in the "Basle Concordat" of 1975 that supervisory responsibility for subsidiaries lies with host country central banks; yet a subsequent recommendation of the same group of central banks provided that banks should be supervised by home country authorities on a globally consolidated basis.[110] Moreover, the Bank of England has specifically stated that "there should not necessarily be considered to be any automatic link between acceptance of responsibility for ongoing supervision and the assumption of a lender-of-last-resort role."[111] In 1983 the Basle group updated the 1975 Concordat, clarifying that both host country and parent country central banks jointly shared responsibility for supervision of branches and subsidiaries with respect to liquidity; and that with respect to solvency, parent central bank supervision applied to branches while joint parent-host supervision applied to subsidiaries. The new policy also explicitly stated, however, that this allocation of jurisdiction applies only to supervision, not lender-of-last-resort responsibility.[112] The LLR loophole thus remains.

To some extent concern about LLR coverage may have been exaggerated. Most US loans through the Eurocurrency market are handled through London branches of US banks, not subsidiaries.[113] Subsidiaries do play a significant

---

109. See, for example, Jack Gutentag and Richard Herring, "The Lender-of-Last-Resort Function in an International Context," *Princeton Essays In International Finance,* no. 151 (Princeton, NJ: Princeton University, May 1983). By contrast, the Group of Thirty has judged the international LLR network to be adequate. Group of Thirty, *Balance of Payments Problems of Developing Countries* (New York: Group of Thirty, 1981), pp. 11–12.

110. Richard S. Dale, Statement Before the Committee on Banking, Finance, and Urban Affairs, US House of Representatives, April 20, 1983.

111. W. P. Cooke, "Developments in Cooperation Among Banking Supervisory Authorities," *Bank of England Quarterly Review,* vol. 21, no.2 (June 1981), pp. 234–44.

112. *IMF Survey* (Washington, July 11, 1983), pp. 201–4.

113. Based on interviews with private bank officials, London, June 1982.

role in some cases, such as subsidiaries of German banks operating in Luxembourg.

The simplest way conceptually, but not necessarily politically, to cover possible gaps in LLR coverage would be to obtain joint agreement by all offshore lending countries (United Kingdom, Luxembourg, Panama, Singapore, the Bahamas, and so on) that they would make it a legal requirement that the parent bank stand behind its foreign subsidiary. The Bank of England already requires nonbinding letters of comfort to this effect. Making the requirement legally binding would ensure the same chain of backing that exists in the case of branches: subsidiary to parent, parent to its home central bank. Parallel action by all offshore countries could avoid central bank unwillingness to adopt this measure because of fear of loss to competitive centers.

Some authorities maintain that a legally binding obligation of parents to subsidiaries, or more generally a clarification by central banks of exactly who would bear LLR responsibility in the case of subsidiaries, would pose the problem of "moral hazard," encouraging reckless action by providing excessive assurance of backing. This argument is not persuasive: any domestic US bank knows that if a central bank is to support it, the Federal Reserve is that central bank; yet the knowledge of this designation causes no moral hazard because the parent bank cannot be assured of support regardless of its actions. While the moral hazard argument appears unfounded, closer supervision of foreign subsidiaries by parent country banks would be necessary under a binding parent bank responsibility; however, the recent approach of global consolidation in supervision is already moving in this direction.

A different type of objection to mandatory parent backing of subsidiaries is that it might be viewed by host governments as infringement on their sovereignty over the subsidiaries. Foreign central banks of parent companies could hardly be expected to be the LLR of the subsidiaries without exercising substantial supervision over them (a trend already in process under global consolidation of capital adequacy tests). Yet, despite the newly reformulated concordat, that supervision might be seen by the host country as undermining the principle of its sovereignty over the subsidiaries (an already sensitive principle in view of issues arising in the area of economic sanctions against the Soviet Union, for example). As an alternative to mandatory parental backing, therefore, a host country could insist that foreign bank subsidiaries be converted to branches, for which there would be no problem of either parental backing or potential undermining of host-country sovereignty (because in the case of branches host countries do not assert sovereignty in the first place).

For some observers, the collapse of the Banco Ambrosiano subsidiary in Luxembourg is evidence of the danger of inadequate LLR coverage. However, because it was a holding company rather than a fully owned subsidiary, and because malfeasance rather than normal business loss appears to have been involved, the Luxembourg Banco Ambrosiano case is not a pure test of the problem of LLR coverage of subsidiaries.

More generally, it would indeed appear that loopholes exist in lender-of-last-resort coverage. However, experience to date suggests that the international financial system has less to fear from a series of bank failures attributable to such loopholes than from straightforward exposure risk of banks whose LLR coverage is not in doubt but whose country loans are. Moreover, the events of 1982–83 illustrate a willingness of central banks to work together in crisis, suggesting that if necessary they could agree on the division of LLR responsibility for currently ambiguous cases.

6   Policy Measures for Capital Flows

The viability of developing country debt over the medium term will depend in part on the availability of new lending from abroad. A central vehicle in financing will be the International Monetary Fund. An examination of prospective financing needs in comparison with prospective availability of funds from this and other potential sources can provide an idea of the feasibility of debt management in the next few years.

IMF Quotas

The policy debate in the United States in recent months has centered on whether there should be an increase in IMF quotas, which provide the primary basis for its lending capacity. Although many countries had called for a doubling of quotas, until the fall of 1982 the Reagan administration opposed a substantial increase.[114] Then, after the dimensions of the debt problem became evident in the Mexican crisis, the administration advanced a proposal it had been considering, to raise the amount available for lending in the IMF

---

114. *Washington Post*, 7 September 1982.

General Arrangements to Borrow (GAB) and to open eligibility for its use as an "emergency fund" for all members of the IMF. Eventually the administration agreed to an increase of 47 percent in IMF quotas (from a base of SDR 61 billion, or approximately $67 billion to SDR 90 billion) combined with an increase in the General Arrangements to Borrow from $6 billion to $19 billion.[115] By August of 1983 both the US Senate and the House of Representatives had passed separate versions of the proposal, but the final bill still required resolution of differences in conference between the two houses as well as passage of appropriations legislation. The House bill passed only narrowly, and only after the inclusion of several restrictive amendments, many of them aimed at tightening regulation of banks.

Throughout the 1950s up to the early 1970s, IMF quotas amounted to about 10 percent of world trade. Today they are only 4 percent.[116] It would be important to raise IMF quotas even if there were no debt problem. In the current environment, it is doubly important to raise IMF resources. If the IMF is to have the influence it needs to induce countries to adopt appropriate policies, it must have sufficient resources to make their participation in such programs attractive. Moreover, with smaller IMF resources banks must bear a higher share of lending and countries must adopt more drastic measures to compensate for lower resource availability. Furthermore, industrial countries as well as developing countries have borrowed from the IMF; the United States itself did so in 1978, and the United Kingdom and Italy have also been large borrowers. In a historical perspective, then, there is an acute need for increased IMF resources.

A more specific evaluation of the inadequacy of IMF resources can be made by comparing its available resources with potential needs.[117] At present the IMF has approximately $35 billion in available, lendable resources ($15 billion in lendable currencies, unused credit lines of $6 billion in the General Arrangements to Borrow, $2 billion in the supplementary financing facility, $8 billion in the enlarged access facility financed largely by borrowing from

---

115. Agreement in principle was reached in November 1982. *Washington Post,* 21 November 1982.

116. IMF *International Financial Statistics,* various issues.

117. The data for the following analysis are drawn primarily from IMF *International Financial Statistics,* various issues. Note that an analysis reaching similar conclusions on IMF resource availability appears in Group of Thirty, *The IMF and the Private Markets* (New York: Group of Thirty, 1983).

Saudi Arabia, and $4 billion in SDRs in the General Account). The amount available to lend varies, depending not only on loans made but also on whether particular currencies are considered sufficiently strong to be made available for lending. Outstanding commitments not yet drawn upon (including the large recent programs for Argentina, Brazil, and Mexico) amount to $19 billion. Thus, the IMF's remaining available resources amount to approximately $16 billion, of which $6 billion is available only for GAB industrial countries. The remaining $10 billion probably should be held largely in reserve, and if it were used when called upon it could be more than exhausted by just three countries borrowing 450 percent of quota: Venezuela, Indonesia, and Nigeria. The proposed increase in IMF quotas by nearly 50 percent plus expansion of the General Arrangements to Borrow would add approximately $29 billion to resources available for lending, giving a total of nearly $40 billion.

US congressional reaction to the proposed IMF quota increase has been mixed. Many legislators have argued that the funds could be better used to address unemployment at home, and that the measure would be a bailout for the banks.

But an international financial collapse would cause far more unemployment inside the United States than might be caused by allocation of resources to the IMF. Indeed, the true cost of the contribution is extremely low. The US contribution would be $8.4 billion. Of this amount, $5.6 billion would be for the quota increase and $2.8 billion for the increase in the GAB. Of the quota increase, 25 percent would be paid in SDRs or other currencies (nondollar, for the United States) specified by the IMF, at zero interest. The other 75 percent would be provided only as called upon, and when called, it would earn remuneration at 85 percent of the SDR interest rate. At current interest rates, the net interest loss on the quota contribution would average about 3.6 percent, for an annual cost of $200 million—an extremely low price for international financial insurance. There would be minimal interest losses on funds lent through the GAB because borrowers would pay rates comparable to US borrowing costs.

As for the argument that the IMF "bails out the banks," it is by now clear that the IMF has been successfully pressuring the banks to continue lending, far from financing their withdrawal. If this charge is meant to convey that without IMF action the banks would experience losses, then the more relevant question becomes whether the general public would truly benefit if the absence of IMF action precipitated avoidable debt collapses that caused such bank losses. It is difficult to conceive of scenarios in which the banks would be forced to absorb losses during financial crisis without causing losses as well for the general public outside of bank stockholders, indeed, probably much larger losses than those of the banks themselves considering the effect of bank leveraging. In addition, some legislators have criticized bank irresponsibility, but the analysis of sections 1 and 2 should make clear that the bulk of today's external debt problem is much more attributable to international economic shocks than to irresponsible behavior of banks.

Even if IMF quotas are increased by the intended 47 percent, and even with a $19 billion emergency fund, IMF resources may prove to be too small. Policymakers should be prepared to support IMF borrowing in private capital markets if necessary,[118] and from individual governments such as Saudi Arabia, Germany, Japan, and the United States. In addition, the IMF must be prepared to go beyond its own internal ceilings on lending to individual countries, in the cases of the "super debtors" that must be kept on track if the system is not to be in severe jeopardy.

Opponents also argue that the IMF should sell its holdings of gold, worth approximately $40 billion at market prices, or borrow in private capital markets, to raise resources rather than receive additional quota contributions from member countries. Compared with quota increases, however, either of these options would tend to reduce the financial strength of the IMF. While that result is undoubtedly consistent with the agenda of some political groups, it is difficult to see how movement in this direction could avoid erosion of the already limited infrastructure for addressing international economic problems.

Financing Requirements

In 1982 severe strain on the international financial system occurred as private banks cut back their net new lending to non-OPEC developing countries, from $43.2 billion in 1981 to only $26.5 billion.[119] The central question is whether there will be sufficient new bank lending, in the medium term, to

---

118. See Group of Thirty, "The IMF and Private Markets" advocating this approach.

119. Calculated from BIS, *The Maturity Distribution International Bank Lending*, (Basle, July 1983, June 1982, and June 1981). The BIS data also show that new bank lending to noncapital-surplus OPEC countries rose from $2.1 billion in 1981 to $5.6 billion in 1982, while the banks actually reduced exposure to Eastern Europe (excluding the Soviet Union) by $1.8 billion in 1981 and $5.8 billion in 1982.

TABLE 20 **Current account balance of nonoil developing countries, 1982–86**
(billion dollars)

Projections	1982	1983	1984	1985	1986
IMF projections	−86.8	−68.0	n.a.	n.a.	−93.0
This study					
16 countries	−44.7	−39.3	−33.0	−27.4	−27.0
Nonoil LDCs[a]	−86.8	−76.3	−64.1	−53.2	−52.5
Morgan Guaranty					
8 countries	−33.3	−19.4	n.a.	−13.3	n.a.
Nonoil LDCs[a]	−86.8	−50.6	n.a.	−34.7	n.a.

n.a. Not available.
Source: IMF *World Economic Outlook,* 1983, p. 205; section 3, this study; and *World Financial Markets,* June 1983, p. 9.
a. Applying 1982 ratio of subgroup to total.

finance even reduced developing-country deficits that are consistent with acceptable domestic growth.

The adequacy of financing may be examined by comparing projected deficits with prospective sources of financing. The International Monetary Fund has projected that the current account deficit of nonoil developing countries will decline from $86.8 billion in 1982 to $68 billion in 1983 and then rise again, to $93 billion by 1986. However, as shown in table 20, on the basis of projections for 16 major nonoil developing countries (including Mexico) in section 3 of this study the total deficit would be considerably less by 1986, only $53 billion. A recent study by Morgan Guaranty bank implies even lower nonoil developing country deficits by this period (table 20).

The analysis of section 3 of this study would suggest that in addition to nonoil developing countries (including Mexico and Ecuador, following IMF definitions), some OPEC countries will need to borrow substantial amounts. For 1986 the base-case estimate of the current account deficit just for Algeria, Indonesia, and Venezuela is $26 billion (a figure that is probably too high because actual adjustment in all likelihood will have to be greater than assumed in the projections). Considering these various estimates, a central figure for developing-country borrowing needs (including the three OPEC countries just mentioned) would be on the order of $75 billion to $80 billion on average in each of the next few years (although the figure would be higher

TABLE 21   **Prospective annual net financing, selected OPEC[a] and nonoil developing countries, 1983–86**
(billion dollars)

	Case A	Case B
Official transfers	14	13
New direct investment	12	10
Official lending		
Concessional	10	10
Nonconcessional		
Multilateral development banks	8	7
IMF	7	2
Official export credits	4	3
Private lending	25	10
Total	80	55

OPEC Organization of Petroleum Exporting Countries.
a. Noncapital-surplus.

if the IMF estimates are accepted, and lower if the Morgan Guaranty estimates are adopted).

Possible levels of average annual financing for 1983–86 are shown in table 21, by source. Official transfers, concessional lending, and net direct investment are all based on 1982 levels with a small allowance for inflation.[120] Levels of multilateral lending and official export credits are similarly based on recent levels and some allowance for inflation and real expansion.[121] In the table, the high alternative, Case A, assumes that banks maintain modest net lending of $25 billion, equivalent to annual expansion of exposure by approximately 7 percent. Case B assumes instead that new bank lending is only $10 billion yearly (an extremely low level that would go little beyond "involuntary lending" for a few major debtor countries). In optimistic Case A, the IMF quota increase is adopted and, with approximately $40 billion in new lendable resources and a normal period of five years between increases,

120. IMF *World Economic Outlook*, 1983, p. 194.

121. OECD, *Development Cooperation 1982*, pp. 206, 233. Note that the World Bank (excluding IDA) accounts for the bulk of multilateral net disbursements. As discussed below, its net lending reached $4.5 billion in 1982, and for 1983–86 the level might be on the order of $6 billion annually.

the IMF lends $7 billion net per year. In pessimistic Case B, the quota increase is not adopted and the IMF lends only $2 billion per year.

The hypothetical levels of financing shown in table 21 indicate that if higher IMF resources become available as planned, and if private bank lending reverts to a slightly higher but still moderate rate, it should be just barely possible to secure the approximately $75 billion to $80 billion in capital that should be required by nonoil developing countries and noncapital-surplus OPEC countries annually in this period. However, if bank lending slows still further and higher IMF resources are not obtained (Case B), financing will be inadequate to cover even the moderate capital needs of developing countries despite their adjustment efforts and their improved positions during world recovery. Thus, the stakes are high for obtaining the IMF quota increase and for pursuing policies that enhance rather than cut off private bank flows.

This analysis also has implications for multilateral development lending. If the capital of the multilateral development banks could be expanded so that their lending rates could rise by 50 percent over this period, they could contribute approximately $4 billion additional net lending annually, or between 5 percent and 7 percent of total net capital flow. Such an increase would be a valuable contribution, especially if private bank financing were low. Accordingly, expansion of multilateral bank lending warrants early attention, although mobilizing the necessary political support will not be easy.

The multilateral banks could also provide more capital in the next three to five years by accelerating the disbursement rate on their loans. Because of long lags in project-loan disbursements, net flows from these agencies are significantly below loan commitment levels. Thus, in 1982 the World Bank made new loan commitments of $10.3 billion and received principal repayments of $1.8 billion. But its net disbursements were only $4.5 billion, far less than the difference between commitments and repayments, because of the multiyear lag in disbursement schedules. Gross disbursements were only $6.3 billion, or 61 percent of commitments.[122] There is a strong case, at least until the firm establishment of international economic recovery, for acceleration of World Bank disbursements. For this purpose a more pronounced movement toward program lending through structural adjustment loans, rather than project lending, would be desirable. Accelerated disbursement does transfer resource availability from the future to the present, but this reallocation would be highly desirable in light of the current global

122. World Bank, *Annual Report 1982*, pp. 10–11, 53, 148.

financial situation (and the still shocked credit markets), especially in those countries where substantial improvement in the external sector is anticipated over the medium term (such as Brazil, section 3). The World Bank could more consciously use variations in its disbursement rate and utilization of structural adjustment loans to play a countercyclical role in the world economy. (At present its role may even be pro-cyclical, aggravating recessionary effects, because its disbursements are linked to tandem funding by the recipient country, and this funding tends to dry up during financial stress.)

Developing-Country Growth

The stress on international debt and cutbacks in lending have already taken a large toll on developing-country growth. Largely because of austerity measures and lower external demand associated with world recession and reductions in international lending, average growth rates of nonoil developing countries have fallen from 5 percent in 1973–80 to 2.4 percent in 1981 and only 0.9 percent in 1982.[123] In Latin America a depression of 1930s magnitude has brought average growth to 1.5 percent in 1981 and −1 percent in 1982.[124] Declines in GNP on the order of 2 percent to 5 percent are expected for Brazil and Mexico in 1983. The influence of the cutback in bank lending in this depression is examined in a study by Morgan Guaranty Bank, which calculates that the decline by approximately $25 billion in bank lending in 1982 translated into a loss of 1½ percentage points in developing-country growth; in turn, slower growth of industrial-country exports to developing countries cut one half of a percentage point off of industrial-country growth.[125]

Critics of IMF adjustment programs sometimes charge that by telling each country individually to reduce imports, the IMF pursues a fallacy of composition, because not all countries' imports can decline at the same time, and their collective attempt to make imports fall will cause world recession.

---

123. IMF *World Economic Outlook*, 1983, p. 171.

124. UN Economic Commission for Latin America, *Preliminary Balance of the Latin American Economy in 1982*, p. 12.

125. *World Financial Markets* (October 1982).

This critique contains two flaws. The first is the implicit assumption that countries in difficulty have any alternative to reducing their trade deficits. They do not, because their financing is limited.[126] The second is the failure to recognize that the magnitude of the trade cutback required—$25 billion to offset decreased bank lending—is small relative to aggregate OECD trade (about $1.5 trillion), and that such a cutback need not induce world recession if there is even a modicum of shift of macroeconomic policy toward expansion in industrial countries.

Moreover, the specific forecasts of this study suggest that for the period 1984–86 resumed growth in developing countries should be compatible with improving debt indicators. Thus, the projections of section 3 assume developing-country growth rising steadily from 2½ percent in 1983 to 4½ percent in 1986. Thus, although the debt burden has already taken a large toll on developing-country growth, there are good prospects for more favorable performance over the medium term—if economic recovery in the industrial countries is achieved.

7 Radical Reform and Contingency Measures

Most analysts agree that orderly servicing of external debt of developing and East European countries will be contingent on world economic recovery in 1983–86. But a number go further: they argue that the debt is already unmanageable and that, either regardless of the extent of world recovery or because they expect it to be weak, the only way to defuse the systemic threat of the debt is to reduce its real burden for developing countries. Their plans

---

126. If the IMF typically lent considerably less than its quota-based ceiling to borrowing countries, and if it had large unused resources, the critique would have more force. The IMF could then vary its practice to require more stringent adjustment with less lending for an individual country during global business cycle expansion, but to permit less stringent adjustment with more financing for the same country when it was borrowing along with many other countries in the midst of global recession. But in practice the IMF has been lending its full limit to countries in difficulty and its resources are slim, ruling out the option of more moderate adjustment with higher lending despite justification on global cyclical grounds.

typically involve an internationally coordinated stretchout of the debt and reduction in its interest burden.

This section presents a critical examination of several of the plans for debt reform. As a preferred alternative, the discussion also outlines a strategy for dealing with debt crises, case by case if and when they arise. Because the potential (although not probable) risk is high, contingency analysis of this type is essential.

Reform Proposals

The principal reform proposals under discussion in the United States are those by Peter B. Kenen of Princeton University, Senator Bill Bradley (D-NJ), Congressman Charles E. Schumer (D-NY), and financier Felix Rohatyn. A unique proposal has also been suggested by Norman A. Bailey of the National Security Council. In addition, some British bankers have been calling for new institutional changes, and some other academics and statesmen have proposed variants on the major reform schemes.

The proposal by Peter Kenen[127] (and in many regards the approach advocated by Senator Bradley) would establish a new International Debt Discount Corporation. This agency would buy up developing-country debt held by banks at a discount of 10 cents on the dollar. It would pay the banks in long-term bonds against itself. It would become the creditor of the developing country, taking over the debt in question. It could afford to grant a modest reduction in the interest rate payable by the developing country, because of the 10 percent discount at which the debt would be purchased from banks. In addition, the agency would renegotiate the debt to longer maturities.

Under Kenen's plan, all banks would be given a limited period of time to decide whether to participate. Once the closing date was reached, subscribers would have no choice among country loans to be sold off: they would exchange all loans for any countries participating in the program. (Otherwise banks would sell off only the weakest loans.) Banks that did not choose to participate by the closing date would not be eligible thereafter to sell their loans to the corporation.

Felix Rohatyn has proposed a related reform measure. Drawing on the

---

127. *New York Times,* 6 March 1983. A variant on this theme appears in Leslie Weinert, "Banks and Bankruptcy," *Foreign Policy,* no. 50 (Spring 1983), pp. 138–49.

analogy of a worldwide Municipal Assistance Corporation—the entity created to revive New York City from bankruptcy—he proposes that developing-country debt be stretched out to long-term maturities of 15 to 30 years, and its interest reduced to perhaps 6 percent.[128] The schedule of principal repayments would be designed so that interest plus principal payments would be no more than 25 percent or 30 percent of exports annually. The vehicle for this conversion would be the International Monetary Fund, the World Bank, or a totally new agency. Such an agency would buy the claims of the banks with long-term bonds it would issue. Rohatyn recognizes that the conversion to long-term, low-interest loans would impose a loss on banks, and that the divison of the loss between bank stockholders, taxpayers, and countries would have to be resolved. He argues that against this loss, banks would achieve greater security of their assets, and that regulators could permit them to spread out their write-downs over a long period of time. Rohatyn also envisions the need for the US government to be prepared to purchase preferred shares in banks as a means of providing them with an infusion of capital in the event that foreign countries seek to intimidate the United States with financial blackmail by threatening outright repudiation of debt.

Congressman Schumer has proposed the conversion of bank loans to long-term, low-interest loans, with the guidance of the IMF.[129] This conversion would be managed directly by the banks and debtor countries, with no new international intermediary: the banks would still be the creditors. Where such conversion is not agreed between the banks and the country, the US executive director in the IMF would be instructed to vote against any IMF loans. The conversion program would set repayments at a manageable fraction of export earnings. Schumer's plan also calls for increased loan-loss reserves when debts are not paid on time—unless restructuring is part of an IMF-negotiated conversion of short-term to long-term loans; establishment of an insurance fund with a small surcharge on renegotiated debt; and country ceilings on short-term loans.

Norman Bailey of the US National Security Council has proposed that developing-country debt be replaced with a form of equity asset ("exchange participation note") entitling the holder to a specified share in the country's

128. Testimony by Felix Rohatyn before the Committee on Foreign Relations, US Senate, Washington, January 17, 1983.

129. See, for example, *Journal of Commerce,* 13 April 1983, and *New York Times,* 10 March 1983.

export earnings.[130] Congressman Andrew Jacobs, Jr., (D-Ind.) has proposed the "Reckless Risk Recovery Act of 1983," which would require that banks owning loans to countries that do not meet payment schedules and which subsequently receive loans from the US government or the IMF reimburse the US Treasury for a pro rata share of such loans.[131]

Certain British bankers (including officials of Barclays Bank and Morgan Grenfell) have advocated a discounting device whereby banks could sell off their rescheduled developing-country debts to central banks or other agencies in order to obtain liquidity for use in other lending, domestic and foreign.[132] Such purchases by central banks could be in the form of bonds issued to the private banks, eligible for discounting for cash if the banks experienced illiquidity. In some versions those bonds would bear no interest so that their eventual sale would only be at a significant discount, causing a loss for the bank—and reflecting the sentiment that banks should pay the price for mistaken loans.

Gutentag and Herring of the University of Pennsylvania have proposed a package of reform measures.[133] Banks would be forced to "mark to market" the foreign loans on their books, making banks more cautious about foreign lending. They could sell off loans at a market rate to the IMF, World Bank, or a new entity, which would combine them with similar loans of other banks and resell to the public participations in the pool (similarly to the Federal Home Loan Mortgage Corporation). Countries in difficulty could convert their loans to consols (where principal is never repaid) at market interest rates. If they missed interest payments, the value of the loan would

---

130. Norman A. Bailey, "A Safety Net for Foreign Lending," *Business Week,* 10 January 1983, p. 17; and in "The International Financial Crisis: An Opportunity for Constructive Action," ed. T. de Saint Phalle (Washington: Georgetown University Center for Strategic and International Studies, 1983), pp. 27–36.

131. US Congress, House, *Reckless Risk Recovery Act of 1983,* H.R. 2069, 98 Cong., 1st sess. (March 11, 1983).

132. Janet Porter, "Answers to Liquidity Crisis Sought," *Journal of Commerce,* 17 March 1983; Barnaby J. Feder, "The World Banking Crisis: Phase Two," *New York Times,* 27 March 1983.

133. Jack Gutentag and Richard Herring, "Overexposure of International Banks to Country Risk: Diagnosis and Remedies," testimony before the US Congress, House Committee on Banking, Finance, and Urban Affairs, Subcommittee on International Trade, Investment, and Monetary Policy, 98 Cong., 1st sess., April 26, 1983.

be marked down in the banks' book by 1 percent for each month's interest missed.

A different genre of proposals would provide insurance for new international lending rather than converting existing debt.[134] Some of these proposals seek to build on the relative popularity of export credit by developing new insurance vehicles based on existing official export credit agencies. Although insurance mechanisms warrant consideration, a fundamental question remains as to whether the public would be prepared to make available through insurance schemes funds that it is unprepared to provide in more traditional forms such as multilateral lending.

Evaluation

Most of the proposals for sweeping debt reform share the following flaws.

DIAGNOSIS   The proposals typically diagnose the current debt situation as unmanageable. In effect, they judge the developing countries to be insolvent, not just illiquid. But unless world economic conditions are depressed for the next three or four years, this debt should be manageable, as analyzed in section 3.

ADVERSE IMPACT   Most of the proposals constitute a counterproductive, panic-based action that would tend to turn good debt into bad debt. Several

---

134. Financier Minos Zombanakis has proposed that rescheduling countries make 13-year agreements with the IMF, and that after 10 years a country unable to service its debt, despite complete adherence to the IMF program, would have its payments guaranteed by the IMF for years 11 through 13. However, the great uncertainty concerning country adherence to IMF programs for a decade, in light of the experience of difficulty of adherence even for months, raises considerable doubt that lenders would take such a program seriously, even if the IMF were prepared to accept such responsibilities. *The Economist*, 30 April 1983, pp. 7–16. British ex-minister Harold Lever has proposed that the official export credit agencies establish an international agency to insure new bank lending, with IMF advice. He suggests large magnitudes of insured lending: $40 billion to $60 billion annually. *The Economist*, 9 July 1983, pp. 14–16. William H. Bolin of the Bank of America and Jorge del Canto, formerly of the IMF, have similarly proposed a new Export Development Fund, loosely linked to the World Bank, to make long-term loans to developing countries for capital equipment imported from industrial countries. The loans would be guaranteed by the official export credit agencies of industrial countries. William H. Bolin and Jorge del Canto, "LDC Debt: Beyond Crisis Management," *Foreign Affairs* (Summer 1983), pp. 1099–1112.

of the schemes would tend to choke off new bank lending to LDCs. Few banks will be prepared to lend new money if the likelihood is high that such money will be subsequently mandated into a program requiring the loss of 10 cents on the dollar, or converted into a low-interest asset. This risk would exist for any bank subscribing to Kenen's International Debt Discount Corporation, because countries currently not suspected to be in trouble could subsequently sign up for the corporation's debt discounting. Perhaps even more important in the current context, *the transfer of bank claims from countries to an international agency would eliminate the incentive for new involuntary lending* as analyzed in section 4. Thus, banks holding claims on Brazil and Mexico are presently lending more to shore up the security of their outstanding loans. But if these claims were transferred to an international agency, this incentive for lending new money to Brazil and Mexico would disappear. Yet the choking-off of new loans would precipitate precisely the crisis that the authors of such proposals fear. Countries such as Brazil need more than a stretchout of existing loans: they need infusions of new loans to cover at least a major portion of the interest due on old loans. Most of the reform proposals would make sense only in an environment in which no new loans whatsoever are expected but maturities are being lengthened; they do not address the need for new lending.

IMPACT ON BANK CAPITAL   Several of the proposals appear naive in that they do not address their dire implications for bank capital. Even a 10 percent write-off of developing country and East European debt would mean a 30 percent cut in capital for the large banks (or somewhat less, allowing for profits and tax effects). More ambitious debt relief such as Rohatyn's and Schumer's would quite likely cause bank losses to exceed capital.

REQUIREMENT OF PUBLIC CAPITAL   New international agencies would have to have massive capital to take over significant developing-country debt. If only half the approximately $700 billion debt were taken over, and if capital backing were full, and if paid-in capital were 10 percent of total, industrial countries would have to authorize contingent liability for $350 billion and actually pay in $35 billion to give an international agency capital backing to take over the debt. Such magnitudes are far beyond any contributions made to multilateral institutions in recent years. As for Schumer's proposal, which does not involve an international agency, it is extraordinary in requiring an outright loss by banks, without providing them in return even the increased security that would be achieved by switching their claims from developing countries to an official entity.

MORAL HAZARD   The establishment of a new international entity to stretch out maturities of developing-country debt and reduce its interest burden would inevitably pose serious "moral hazard" problems of inducing changes in action that are to the self-interest of the debtor at the expense of the creditor and taxpayer. With such an entity in place there would be a strong incentive for any developing country to seek debt relief even when it would be possible with appropriate adjustment policies to continue to meet orderly debt payments. Such an incentive would result even from maturity stretchout, which would be less injurious (if at all) to banks; it would be extremely strong if in addition there were substantial reduction in the interest rate owed (by far the more damaging feature for creditors). It would be a structural flaw in the system to build in an incentive to debt-servicing disruption. It is for this reason that debt reschedulings have typically been carried out only when the alternative was imminent default.

Some of the specific proposals vary from the central theme of the Kenen-Bradley-Rohatyn-Schumer approaches but involve other difficulties. Bailey's exchange participation notes would seem unlikely to receive much acceptance in markets because of the limited credibility of being able to enforce a claim on a certain fraction of the country's export earnings. In the Gutentag and Herring approach, it is unclear why banks voluntarily would sell off sovereign loans at a deep discount as long as chances remained for greater recovery, and in the absence of a wide market for such sales it would be arbitrary for regulators to impose a low market valuation to which these assets would be marked. As for converting country loans to consols, it is unclear why countries should be given an infinite leash, even if the typical rescheduling leash of one to two years is too short.

Contingency Planning

Given the current outlook for the world economy and developing-country debt, it would be far better to have emergency plans in reserve than to set up sweeping new reform mechanisms that could make the problem worse than need be. The general strategy of contingency planning should be something along the following lines. Debt problems should continue to be handled case by case. When a country gets into trouble there should be negotiations between it and its private and public creditors. It is quite possible that some of the negotiated reschedulings already concluded will come unstuck, perhaps including one or more of the rescue packages arranged for the super-debtors.

If the conventional reschedulings and rescue packages are insufficient, the first line of defense would be to repeat the package but with an additional round of support from the key participants: private banks, industrial-country governments (through such instruments as Federal Reserve swap loans, agricultural credits, and export agency loans), and the IMF. In even more extreme cases it may be necessary to have banks capitalize some portion of the interest otherwise due into additional principal due in future years. The national regulatory authorities could treat such capitalized interest as not causing classification of the loans as nonperforming, provided that there were a coherent, IMF-supported adjustment program. However, the banks in this case would appropriately set aside provisions for the amount of interest rescheduled, rather than reporting it as accrued income available for distribution to shareholders. In even worse cases, it could be necessary for creditors to enter some arrangement analogous to bankruptcy proceedings, whereby creditors would seek to collect only some fraction of the debt over a prescribed period.

The central point is that the resolution of such contingency cases would be addressed in a negotiating context case by case without setting up international machinery that would cause perverse incentives for unnecessary default.

One possible innovation that warrants consideration is the use of "zero coupon bonds" as an instrument for lending without imposing an immediate interest burden. Like US savings bonds, zero coupon bonds pay no interest until maturity. They are redeemed at a fixed, stated value and their initial sales price is discounted accordingly, so that they yield a market rate of return (but pay the return only at maturity). Zero coupon bonds have the merit of being a normal capital-market asset that would nonetheless accomplish the delay of interest payment to a later date when a country's external position is expected to be much stronger. The alternative of rescheduling interest on existing loans would accomplish the same economic effect but would raise problems of market psychology as well as of regulatory response.

The preferable use of zero coupon bonds would be as the vehicle for new loans to a country in difficulty. Thus, instead of making new loans to a country for seven years at annual interest of LIBOR plus 1½ percent (for example), banks could instead purchase zero coupon bonds from the country in comparable amounts.[135]

---

135. Because the bond would bear a fixed payment, this innovation would involve moving the banks back to the fixed-interest basis of their lending before the advent of variable-interest loans (linked to LIBOR) in the mid-1970s. Conceivably zero coupon bonds could be designed to bear variable interest, but for purposes of applying accepted capital market instruments it would probably be preferable merely to revert to bank assumption of the risk of interest fluctuation.

A less attractive alternative, but one that might have to be considered in more extreme circumstances, would be to convert existing loans into zero coupon bonds (technically, by simultaneously having the country prepay the loans and issue zero coupon bonds). The disadvantage of such conversion of past loans is that it would be extremely close to the deferral of interest on existing loans, a step that triggers classification of loans as nonperforming. Of course, it would be even better to remain with the normal types of bank financing; but as a contingency strategy, when the alternative might be moratorium, zero coupon bonds warrant attention.

8   Policy Conclusions

The central conclusion of this study is that with reasonable recovery in the global economy, the problem of international debt should prove manageable and the degree of its current risk to the international system should decline. The adoption of appropriate macroeconomic policies to ensure global recovery is therefore important not only in its own right but also because of the debt problem.

A Balanced Strategy

The external debt situation clearly poses a potential risk to the international financial system. The nine largest US banks have nearly 300 percent of their capital exposed in loans to developing and East European countries. One of the two largest US banks has 74 percent of its equity capital exposed in Brazil and another 55 percent in Mexico. Approximately two-thirds of the value of outstanding bank loans to developing and East European countries is owed by countries that have experienced some form of disruption in their debt servicing within the last year. And even under the broadly favorable base-case outlook (section 3), capital flows of $75 billion to $80 billion annually will be required and countries accounting for one-fourth of total debt (primarily oil exporters) will experience deterioration in their debt-servicing burden.

Despite this systemic risk, a measured policy response is the best course. Overreaction by banks, public officials, or borrowing countries could make matters far worse. In particular, some of the more sweeping policy proposals for global debt reform could prove counterproductive.

The basic policy strategy recommended in this study is as follows. The root cause of the current debt problem is global recession. Country adjustment programs with IMF and other official support—such as the rescue programs for Argentina, Brazil, and Mexico in 1982–83—should continue to be the basic approach to interim management of the debt problem until the natural improvement associated with international economic recovery can take effect. Progress under the key rescue packages has been impressive to date, although in Brazil the process of coming to grips with severe budgetary imbalances and inflationary pressure is still evolving, and technical problems in the external financing package require correction. Broadly, the debt problem is one of illiquidity, not insolvency, and if sufficient financial packages can be arranged to tide over debtor countries temporarily, they should be able to return to a sound financial footing within two to four years.

However, some major borrowers are unlikely to be able to return swiftly to financial normalcy. Detailed debt projections applying a statistical model based on past debt reschedulings suggest that it may not be until 1985 that Mexico and Argentina can return to normal borrowing from the capital market, or until 1986 for Brazil. Until that time it is essential that continued new lending be extended by banks already exposed, although in relatively moderate amounts (such as 7 percent of exposure annually). Fortunately, the analysis of section 4 suggests that the banks have a strong incentive to continue lending, because modest new lending can ensure that their outstanding loans do not go sour.

To ensure new lending by banks already exposed, the "free-rider" problem, whereby smaller banks seek to avoid bearing their share of extra lending, should be addressed through moral suasion by central banks, pressure from large banks, and incentives by borrowing countries—possibly including subordination of loans of uncooperative banks.

It is central to this broad strategy that the official international financial agencies have sufficient means not only to address the problem but also to provide a psychological climate of competent international management of the debt problem. For this purpose it is essential that the proposed increase in the quotas of the IMF and resources of the General Arrangements to Borrow be implemented as soon as possible. Moreover, this increase should not be accompanied by new regulatory requirements that would choke off new lending. (Although the Senate version of the bill to increase IMF quotas is relatively clean of such measures, the version adopted by the House would impose a seriously punitive requirement to set aside reserves on all rescheduled loans, even though they subsequently fully meet interest and principal payments; see section 5.)[136]

More generally, bank regulatory overkill should be avoided. Regulatory reforms proposed by the Federal Reserve, Comptroller of the Currency, and FDIC strike the appropriate balance between increased prudence and excessive regulatory restrictions. It must be kept in mind that, because new international bank loans have fallen from $43 billion in 1981 to $26 billion in 1982, the current problem is too little lending, not too much. It is misguided to see the debt problem as primarily the result of excessive or irresponsible bank lending; the analysis of section 1 shows the overwhelming role of exogenous shocks in the world economy in creating the current situation (oil price shocks, sharply higher interest rates, and declining export prices and volumes caused by global recession).

In the basic strategy of treating external debt problems as ones of temporary illiquidity rather than insolvency—meaning that public policy adopts temporary lending rather than write-offs or other actions analogous to bankruptcy proceedings—it must be recognized that there may nonetheless be new disruptions ahead. Policymakers should be prepared to deal with such contingencies, including large disruptions. The basic plan for such contingencies should be to remain in a negotiating process with the country. This process should in each case involve additional efforts on the parts of all parties: the country in its adjustment measures, the banks in their additional lending, and industrial-country governments and the IMF in their support. In some cases the IMF may have to exceed its quota-based ceiling on loans to a given country (as it has occasionally done in the past, as in the case of Jamaica). Correspondingly, it would be desirable that after the implementation of the new, higher level of IMF quotas, the country ceiling as a percentage of quota, not be proportionately reduced (at least not fully), to permit some increase in the absolute amounts of IMF resources available to individual countries.

It is essential to this strategy that the creditor-debtor relationship remain in a cooperative mode. Some of the largest debtor countries have large unused bargaining leverage because of their weight relative to bank capital. As long as the basic dynamics of negotiation are cooperative, however, debtors are unlikely to exploit this leverage because of longer run costs of damaging their creditworthiness. Indeed, each country's concern for its own

---

136. US Congress, House Committee on Banking, Finance, and Urban Affairs, *International Recovery and Financial Stability Act*, H.R. 2957, 98 Cong., 1st sess., 1983.

creditworthiness should be a relatively secure safeguard against the emergence of a debtors' cartel with demands for concessional renegotiation.

For this general strategy to work, it will be important that official financing flows be as substantial as possible. Through the 1970s capital flows to developing countries were shifting in composition from official to private, with the result of shortening maturities and rising interest rates. The sluggish response of official lending and strong response of private lending to increased borrowing needs (driven by the oil shock and global macroeconomic conditions) caused this shift, but after the abrupt contraction in private lending associated with debt disruption in 1982–83, it is time for the pendulum to swing back again. Accordingly, the chances for the basic strategy to work will be increased if not only the IMF quota increases are adopted but also larger volumes of lending are provided through the World Bank and other multilateral financial agencies.

It would not appear essential to the strategy recommended here that new institutions be invented. As analyzed in section 7, proposals for stretching out debt and reducing its interest rate through a new international agency would probably be counterproductive, because the result would be to choke off new bank lending (even if the large requirements for public capital could be mobilized). Even a new vehicle for "bridge lending" prior to IMF agreements seems unlikely to be essential, because central banks can act on a case-specific basis (as they have done) when a large debtor country is involved, and if the country is small it can merely go into arrears without jeopardizing the system.

The greatest unknowns in this general strategy are twofold: will international economic recovery be sufficient, and will the political tolerance to austerity programs in developing countries be sufficient to provide time for adjustment measures to work? As is argued in section 3, the prospects seem relatively favorable that the critical threshold of 3 percent OECD growth in 1984–86 will be achieved, although additional macroeconomic policy changes would be desirable to help ensure this outcome.

With respect to political stability, analysts such as Henry A. Kissinger have warned against political breakdown in hard-pressed debtor countries.[137] So far, however, the political response in critical cases has been encouraging. In Brazil the process of political opening continues, despite instances of rioting. In Mexico labor has been remarkably cooperative, to the point of accepting relatively modest wage increases despite high inflation. In Argentina

---

137. Henry A. Kissinger, "Saving the World Economy," *Newsweek*, 24 January 1983.

both major opposition parties appear to recognize that certain elements of financial management will have to be maintained after transition to civilian rule. Although in Chile recent political disruption has been significant, the economic adjustment program there may be less relevant as a cause than long-standing political strains under a military government (that, until now, had based its claim to legitimacy in large part on economic performance).

Successful pursuit of the basic strategy outlined here should alleviate the severe economic recession that has hit the developing countries harder than any since the Great Depression. Largely because of debt and balance of payments pressures, economic growth rates are abysmal. However, under conditions of reasonable world recovery, the calculations of section 3 suggest that the major debtor countries should be able to return to growth rates on the order of 3 percent to 5 percent in 1984–86. Successful orchestration of the lending process outlined here will be a requirement for this outcome, however. Effectively managing the debt crisis will mean not only that jeopardy to the financial system and economies of the North is avoided but also that a return to crucial long-run growth in the South can be achieved.

Summary Recommendations

The analysis of this study leads to several concrete policy recommendations.

STRATEGY   Global economic recovery is essential. More expansionary policies would be desirable in key countries such as Germany, the United Kingdom, and Japan. In the United States, the massive budget deficit looming for several years should be reduced, paving the way for a monetary policy that can reduce interest rates and thereby avoid recessionary spillovers to the rest of the world and undue debt-servicing burdens for developing countries in particular. Similarly, a better fiscal-monetary match is required to reduce overvaluation of the dollar, which also aggravates the debt burden (section 3).

Sweeping debt reform, such as comprehensive programs to stretch out debt and reduce interest rate obligations, should be avoided as counterproductive. New forms of capital flows should be sought to replace declining bank lending in a context where large increases in offical lending will be difficult.

OFFICIAL CAPITAL   Efforts should nonetheless be made to increase lending through multilateral development banks, on an accelerated basis through structural adjustment loans instead of project loans. And it is of paramount importance that the proposed IMF quota increase be adopted promptly.

TRADE POLICY   Another policy implication of this study is that it will be crucial to avoid new protection in industrial-country markets against the exports of developing countries. The prospect of improvement in the relationship of external debt to exports hinges on growing exports from developing countries. If a wave of new protection depresses exports from levels they might otherwise be expected to attain as global recovery proceeds, the prospects for improvement in the problem of international debt will be much more bleak. Tighter import restrictions on textiles and apparel, sugar, and steel are among the disturbing signs of increased protection in industrial countries within the last two years, and these measures have affected the exports of developing (as well as industrial) countries. Nonetheless, industrial-country markets currently remain relatively open to exports from developing countries, and this continued market opportunity will be essential for a favorable resolution to the debt problem. This fact must be kept in mind in all decisions concerning national policy response to new pleas for protection—at a time when protectionist demands are high because of high unemployment and (in the United States) an overvalued dollar that makes domestic production less competitive.[138]

BANKING   The new banking regulations on foreign lending suggested by the Federal Reserve, Comptroller of the Currency, and FDIC, should be adopted. However, more restrictive banking regulations (such as the House version of the IMF quota bill, making all rescheduled loans subject to provisioning) should be avoided because of the severe risk of regulatory overkill that would restrict lending even more at a time when the need is for its recovery. Country lending limits for banks should probably be avoided, although not because country lending is without risk. Lender-of-last-resort capacity should be strengthened by a joint agreement of offshore banking centers to require legally that foreign parent banks stand behind their subsidiaries.

Private banks should continue new lending at modest rates to countries in adjustment. The IMF should continue its important new role of mobilizing

---

138. C. Fred Bergsten and William R. Cline, *Trade Policy in the 1980s*, POLICY ANALYSES IN INTERNATIONAL ECONOMICS 3 (Washington: Institute for International Economics, November 1982).

bank lending actively. Central banks, large private banks, and borrowing countries should take measures to overcome the "free-rider" problem and ensure that smaller banks continue to lend as well.

The new Institute for International Finance should prepare country credit ratings as well as provide banks with information, in order to provide more discipline to the bank-lending process.

RESCHEDULING   Formal rescheduling should generally be relied upon rather than moral suasion unless the borrower is in a strong fundamental position, and reliance on interbank deposits as a form of indirect rescheduling is especially ineffective. Rescheduling for two years or even more is probably preferable to single-year reschedulings. Higher interest rates and fees in rescheduling, within reason, probably facilitate rescheduling by helping mobilize bank support; but because of political reaction in borrowing (and some lending) countries, such increases may have to be more modest than in the recent past. In cases of breakdown in initial rescheduling packages, a contingency approach should be to maintain a cooperative creditor-debtor relationship and to make additional adjustments on the part of each party to the package.

By pursuing the basic strategy outlined here and adopting specific elements recommended for its implementation, it should be possible for the international community to overcome the systemic strains posed by the debt crisis of 1982–83 and to restore more complete stability to the international economy.

Appendices

A. Notes on Data

In addition to the specific data sources cited for individual tables and estimates indicated in the main text of this study, the following data sources warrant mention. Total debt (for example, section 3 and table B-1) is estimated in a variety of ways. The World Bank's *World Debt Tables* provide data on long-term public debt for all of the countries examined, and for long-term private debt in some cases, although this source only covers information through 1981.[1] For 1982 debt, national sources, press reports, and other international official estimates are used.

Total debt is obtained by adding short-term debt to long-term debt. Short-term debt is estimated in the following way using data for 1977–82 from the Bank for International Settlements (BIS).[2] For a given year, these data report the amount of debt coming due within one year (D_t^1) and the amount coming due within the second year (D_t^2). It is possible to isolate short-term debt by subtracting from the total coming due within one year that portion that represents payment on previous long-term debt, as indicated by the principal due in the "second" year as reported in the previous year's data. Thus:

$$D_t^s = D_t^1 - D_{t-1}^2$$

where D_t^s is the estimate of outstanding short-term debt in year t. This approach ignores any short-term debt other than that owed to banks covered by the BIS reporting system.

Because the BIS data on bank debt maturities are unavailable for years before 1977, the estimates of short-term debt for earlier years are based on the ratio of short-term debt in 1978 to imports of goods and services (excluding interest) in that year, as applied to imports of goods and services for earlier years. This procedure assumes that, in 1978 and before, the principal use of short-term debt was as trade finance.

---

1. World Bank, *World Debt Tables* 1982–83 ed.

2. BIS, *The Maturity Distribution of International Bank Lending*, various issues.

The debt-service ratio (table B-1) is defined as the ratio of total interest payments on all debt and amortization of medium- and long-term debt, *divided by* exports of goods and services. (Note that the interest payment concept is gross: interest receipts are not deducted.) The data sources are the International Monetary Fund's data tapes for *Balance of Payments Yearbook* (BOPY), for interest and amortization, and *International Financial Statistics* (IFS), for exports of goods and services.

In table B-1, net debt *equals* the gross debt (including short-term) *minus* nongold reserves. Net debt relative to exports of goods and services is obtained using the data for these exports as just described.

Additional data required for the simulation model of section 3 include amortization rates, share of debt at fixed interest rates, and average rate on fixed-interest debt. These data are based on a variety of sources, including the Bank for International Settlements, the World Bank's *World Debt Tables*, financial press accounts, and the International Monetary Fund. *International Financial Statistics* provides data required for the model on merchandise trade, oil trade, direct foreign investment, transfers, and reserves, and for exports and imports of services the ratios to merchandise trade from the most recent data available in the IMF's *Balance of Payments Yearbook* are used. Country growth rates in the base year 1982 are from regional and official sources.[3]

The terms of trade elasticities in the model of section 3 are based on simple regression estimates, using data for 1961–81. The percentage change in the price index of the country's exports, as deflated by the price index for industrial country exports (*International Financial Statistics*), is related to the change in OECD country growth rate (OECD *Outlook*, various issues).

---

3. UN Economic Commission for Latin America, *Preliminary Balance of the Latin American Economy in 1982* (Santiago, January 1983); Asian Development Bank, *Annual Report 1982* (Manilla, 1982); and IMF staff estimates.

B. Statistical Tables

TABLE B-1 **Debt indicators for 10 large debtor countries, 1973–82**

Country	1973	1974	1975	1976	1977
Total debt[a] (billion dollars)					
Brazil	13.8	18.9	23.3	28.6	35.2
Mexico	8.6	12.8	16.9	21.8	27.1
Argentina	6.4	8.0	7.9	8.3	9.7
Spain	5.7	8.6	10.7	13.5	16.3
Korea	4.6	6.0	7.3	8.9	11.2
Venezuela	4.6	5.3	5.7	8.7	12.3
India	10.5	11.6	12.4	13.4	14.7
Yugoslavia	4.6	5.4	6.3	7.7	9.6
Indonesia	5.7	7.1	8.9	11.0	12.8
Israel	5.9	6.9	7.8	9.0	10.0
Debt service[b]/exports[c] (percentage)					
Brazil	36.7	36.0	40.8	45.3	48.7
Mexico	28.7	21.9	30.3	40.7	53.6
Argentina	19.9	21.3	31.9	26.2	19.1
Spain	5.2	4.2	9.3	10.7	13.3
Korea	11.5	11.8	12.5	9.8	10.2
Venezuela[d]	3.8	3.3	3.5	8.4	10.0
India	23.6	63.7	14.0	11.5	12.3
Yugoslavia	21.7	21.7	21.1	18.3	19.4
Indonesia	3.4	2.1	6.2	7.2	8.3
Israel	21.7	22.4	26.8	24.5	22.2
Net debt[e]/exports[c] (percentage)					
Brazil	106.2	145.9	194.3	195.8	207.6
Mexico	154.6	182.0	243.8	286.5	309.7
Argentina	140.8	145.2	211.5	145.7	96.8
Spain	−4.1	21.0	37.7	60.3	60.3
Korea	88.9	106.5	110.2	73.4	63.0
Venezuela	51.2	−5.9	−37.3	−32.9	−8.7
India	290.7	248.0	200.8	159.9	125.7
Yugoslavia	76.0	75.6	88.8	81.8	100.1
Indonesia	146.9	75.2	118.0	108.9	94.6
Israel	145.5	154.8	173.3	168.9	150.3

n.a. Not available.
a. Including short-term.
b. Interest on long- and short-term debt plus amortization on long-term.

1978	1979	1980	1981	1982
48.4	57.4	66.1	75.7	88.2
33.6	40.8	53.8	67.0	82.0
12.5	19.0	27.2	35.7	38.0
18.4	22.2	27.4	33.2	n.a.
14.8	20.5	26.4	31.2	35.8
16.3	23.7	27.5	29.3	31.3
15.6	15.9	17.7	18.5	n.a.
11.8	14.9	17.6	18.5	n.a.
14.5	14.9	17.0	18.0	21.0
11.6	13.2	15.6	17.9	20.4
59.3	65.6	60.8	66.9	87.1
64.9	67.7	36.4	48.5	58.5
41.6	21.3	32.2	37.5	102.9
19.5	15.7	15.5	19.0	n.a.
12.0	13.9	17.3	18.8	21.1
15.6	16.4	15.6	19.0	20.7
11.4	11.2	n.a.	n.a.	n.a.
21.0	20.8	20.0	n.a.	30.3
9.7	7.4	4.9	5.2	11.3
22.9	22.0	24.6	26.0	23.7
252.5	269.3	259.1	256.6	365.3
278.2	241.7	205.7	209.0	248.6
96.1	97.3	182.5	275.3	353.5
37.4	30.0	46.0	66.2	n.a.
70.2	89.8	103.8	103.9	104.5
35.6	41.5	33.2	29.3	104.2
107.9	81.1	n.a.	n.a.	n.a.
110.4	133.6	118.8	99.8	n.a.
104.7	69.8	52.2	54.9	86.2
131.6	121.8	120.7	132.6	180.9

c. Exports include services.
d. Deduction of interest earnings would make net debt-service ratios much lower.
e. Debt *minus* external official assets, nongold.

TABLE B-2 **Current account and debt projections, selected countries, 1982–86**
(million dollars and ratios)

		1982	1983	1984	1985	1986
Egypt	CA	−2,500	−2,555	−3,033	−3,647	−3,806
	D	18,000	19,699	22,057	24,857	27,699
	NDX	2.398	2.595	2.416	2.457	2.424
Algeria	CA	−2,935	−2,401	−4,824	−5,500	−5,482
	D	15,093	17,136	21,941	27,189	32,320
	NDX	1.283	1.668	2.072	2.561	2.667
Portugal	CA	−2,278	−1,736	−1,312	−1,236	−1,367
	D	12,900	14,538	15,939	17,166	18,530
	NDX	2.030	2.039	1.752	1.650	1.590
Peru	CA	−1,400	−2,260	−2,421	−2,578	−2,799
	D	11,100	13,187	15,427	17,748	20,245
	NDX	2.479	2.769	2.589	2.616	2.698
Thailand	CA	−1,100	−512	338	931	1,339
	D	10,500	10,688	10,207	9,016	7,366
	NDX	1.061	0.972	0.697	0.502	0.330
Romania	CA	−600	407	1,522	2,217	2,501
	D	8,200	8,075	6,947	4,979	2,854
	NDX	0.595	0.497	0.317	0.171	0.038
Hungary	CA	−150	−961	−324	−241	−75
	D	7,500	8,632	9,303	9,797	10,126
	NDX	0.622	0.626	0.523	0.483	0.439
Ecuador	CA	−1,100	−1,243	−1,458	−1,687	−1,808
	D	6,300	7,535	9,017	10,694	12,476
	NDX	1.990	2.330	2.324	2.495	2.591

CA current account; D total debt; NDX net debt (deducting reserves) relative to exports of goods and services.

TABLE B-3 **Base-case projections**
(million dollars and ratios)

	1982	1983	1984	1985	1986
Oil importers					
Exports	110,536	125,243	158,805	179,936	199,758
Oil	0	0	0	0	0
Imports	−125,552	−135,360	−159,308	−174,566	−194,848
Oil	−34,499	−29,426	−29,426	−29,426	−34,499
Services					
Exports	30,442	34,347	43,378	49,138	54,551
Interest	−29,464	−29,256	−30,058	−29,591	−30,187
Other imports	−35,076	−40,691	−50,587	−56,475	−62,444
Transfers	13,057	14,827	17,563	18,994	20,542
Current account	−35,451	−30,890	−20,207	−12,564	−12,626
Direct investment	4,426	5,026	5,953	6,439	6,963
Amortization	−25,612	−31,091	−33,571	−34,927	−35,159
Net loans	23,234	28,218	19,044	9,177	9,719
Gross loans	48,846	59,309	52,615	44,105	44,878
Reserves change	−7,791	2,353	4,790	3,052	4,056
Reserves	25,470	27,823	32,613	35,665	39,721
Total debt	299,377	327,595	346,638	355,816	365,535
Debt service/exports	0.391	0.378	0.315	0.282	0.257
Net debt/exports	1.943	1.878	1.553	1.398	1.281
Current account/exports	−0.251	−0.194	−0.100	−0.055	−0.050
Reserves/imports	0.159	0.158	0.155	0.154	0.154
Oil exporters					
Exports	76,300	69,783	74,836	78,072	89,813
Oil	59,140	50,443	50,443	50,443	59,140
Imports	−64,756	−66,835	−84,013	−92,747	−101,070
Oil	0	0	0	0	0
Services					
Exports	61,261	18,381	23,493	26,771	29,720
Interest	−15,423	−16,520	−16,886	−18,305	−21,284
Other imports	−26,434	−27,075	−34,429	−37,996	−41,391
Transfers	2,249	2,554	3,025	3,272	3,538
Current account	−20,989	−19,711	−33,973	−40,933	−40,674
Direct investment	3,171	3,601	4,265	4,613	4,989

TABLE B-3 **Base-case projections (*Continued*)**
(million dollars and ratios)

	1982	1983	1984	1985	1986
Oil exporters					
Amortization	− 15,925	− 18,408	− 20,136	− 23,467	− 27,248
Net loans	189	16,780	33,144	38,067	37,350
Gross loans	16,114	35,188	53,280	61,535	64,598
Reserves change	− 17,629	670	3,436	1,747	1,665
Reserves	20,930	21,600	25,035	26,782	28,447
Total debt	184,778	201,558	234,702	272,769	310,119
Debt service/exports	0.339	0.396	0.377	0.398	0.406
Net debt/exports	1.770	2.041	2.132	2.346	2.356
Current account/exports	− 0.227	− 0.224	− 0.346	− 0.390	− 0.340
Reserves/imports	0.230	0.230	0.211	0.205	0.200
Nineteen countries					
Exports	186,836	195,026	233,642	258,008	289,571
Oil	59,140	50,443	50,443	50,443	59,140
Imports	− 190,308	− 202,195	− 243,321	− 267,314	− 295,918
Oil	− 34,499	− 29,426	− 29,426	− 29,426	− 34,499
Services					
Exports	46,703	52,728	66,871	75,909	84,272
Interest	− 44,887	− 45,775	− 46,944	− 47,896	− 51,471
Other imports	− 61,510	− 67,766	− 85,016	− 94,471	− 103,835
Transfers	15,306	17,381	20,588	22,266	24,081
Current account	− 56,440	− 50,602	− 54,181	− 53,498	− 53,300
Direct investment	7,597	8,627	10,219	11,051	11,952
Amortization	− 41,537	− 49,500	− 53,707	− 58,395	− 62,407
Net loans	23,423	44,998	52,187	47,245	47,069
Gross loans	64,960	94,497	105,895	105,639	109,476
Reserves change	− 25,420	3,023	8,225	4,799	5,721
Reserves	46,400	49,423	57,648	62,447	68,168
Total debt	484,155	529,153	581,340	628,585	675,654
Debt service/exports	0.370	0.385	0.335	0.318	0.305
Net debt/exports	1.874	1.936	1.743	1.695	1.625
Current account/exports	− 0.242	− 0.204	− 0.180	− 0.160	− 0.143
Reserves/imports	0.184	0.183	0.176	0.173	0.171